The Best Walks in the Shropshire Hills

The Best Walks in the Shropshire Hills

Gillian Walker
Sketches by George Allen

For William - my dog; a good companion and a constant friend.

First published in Great Britain 1989 by Management Update Ltd.
99a Underdale Road Shrewsbury SY2 5EE
Shropshire. (Tel: 0743 232556)

ISBN 0 946679 36 3

Front Cover: Cardingmill Valley, Church Stretton photograph by W. Hopewell LRPS. Back Cover: Beech Avenue, Linley Hill photograph by G. Walker. Other photographs by the author.

Typeset by Litho Link Ltd., Leighton, Welshpool, Powys, Wales.
Printed and bound by Billing & Son Ltd., Worcester.

CONTENTS

Please note that all the routes described in this book use public rights of way as shown on the definitive map current at the time of publication. Whilst every care has been taken to be accurate throughout, the author and the publishers cannot accept responsibility for changes or diversions or extinguishments made or for any misinterpretation by those using this book.

INTRODUCTION

"Into my heart an air that kills
From you far country blows
What are those blue remembered hills,
What spires, what farms are those?

That is the land of lost content
I see it shining plain,
The happy highways where I went
And cannot come again'

A E Housman - 'A Shropshire Lad'

The twenty six walks in this book, though of interest to the experienced rambler and the long distance hill-walker, are mainly aimed at those who are fairly new to walking for pleasure and who may not yet be totally familiar with map and compass or who perhaps feel a little bolder about hills if presented with detailed directions.

Each walk includes the ascent of at least one hill. Disappointingly, not every hill's summit point is crossed by a public footpath but the walks take you as near as possible to the highest point using correct paths.

It is possible to achieve all walks in this book without using a map or compass, although they are valuable aids - not the least in reaching the start along the lanes and by-ways! The most you will find in the way of 'technical' terms are the grid references at the start of each walk for those who wish them and the occasional reference to the general direction, i.e. North, South, East or West. It would be helpful if the walker knew how to interpret a grid reference and to read and use a map and compass, but intelligent and careful use of the descriptions and sketches should see most quite painlessly - and one hopes enjoyably - through all these journeys.

In the unlikely event of your losing your bearings, remember you are not lost; you are merely 'temporarily misplaced'. You are never very far away from 'civilisation' here even though you may feel you are. Most of the natives are friendly enough to set you back on the right track. The worst that may happen to you is that you will arrive home a little late for dinner. However, care is needed when venturing onto the Long Mynd or Stiperstones and whilst no real danger is before you, it would be more enjoyable and less troublesome if you undertook walks in these areas in relatively fine weather; at least until you become more familiar with hills and high wide expanses.

Some may criticise the omission of certain hills in the county such as The Wrekin and Wenlock Edge but unfortunately time and space have their limiting effect.

MAPS The maps which cover the walks in this book are O.S. Landranger Series 1:50000 No. 126 and O.S. Landranger Series 1:50000 No. 137. For larger scale use, the best are O.S. Pathfinder Series 1:25000 Nos. SO 29/39 (Montgomery); SO 47/57 (Ludlow); SO 28/38 (Bishop's Castle & Clun); SO 49/59 (Church Stretton); SO 48/58 (Craven Arms); SO 27/37 (Knighton & Brampton Bryan); SJ 40/50 (Pontesbury) and SJ 41/51 (Shrewsbury).

ANIMALS In Shropshire the most common animal is the sheep although cattle farming is also popular. Generally, cows present no danger at all but they can become rather protective if with calves and it is best not to come between a cow and her calf.
You may find the occasional bull in the field. The law allows farmers to run non-dairy bulls aged under 11 months in a field across which a public footpath may run provided it is with cows. Frankly, no bull is to be trusted and it is best to give them as wide a berth as possible.
Nearly every walk avoids walking through a farmyard. When you do meet farm dogs, most of them, although noisy are friendly. If they bark they are only doing their job and will generally cease their noise when you are off their territory. All animals in the country are either curious or afraid of dogs generally and it is imperative that if one takes one's own dog on these walks that it is kept under close control, which means on a lead most of the time. Even a dog on a lead walking across a field will attract the inquisitive attention of young heifers or bullocks. It is worth remembering that the law permits farmers to shoot any dog which the farmer may have cause to believe is worrying his livestock or putting them in danger.

FOOTPATHS The land over which you walk may belong to the Crown, the Forestry Commission, the National Trust or to private farmers and landowners. The fact is that the land does not belong to us and it is this that I believe many ramblers and walkers would do well to remember. The Ramblers Association and similar groups and bodies who are vigilant watchdogs of our public rights of way do superb work in ensuring that the landowners realise their duties and attend to them, but in protecting our rights of way, some dedicated ramblers behave as though they have forgotten that we are exercising mere rights over land, not acts of ownership! Their arrogance and their militance does them and what they stand for a disservice and rightly upsets many farmers who otherwise would be quite happy to perform their obligations as far as public footpaths are concerned. A farmer is in the business of earning a living and naturally does not put such unproductive work as erecting stiles high on the list of priorities. This does not always mean that a farmer is trying to deter walkers. Living and working as I do in a farming community, I find that contrary to what many town-based ramblers believe, most farmers and landowners are aware of their obligations. They may not always be too diligent in keeping old rights of way open and unobstructed, but they accept the fact of their existence and the right of members of the public to walk them. However, the best is not brought out in even the most reasonable farmers when confronted with jaw-jutting townies demanding their rights, climbing their fences and gates and allowing dogs to upset their stock. *If we always keep in mind the fact that we do not own the land and behave accordingly, we should keep on reasonable terms with all but the most awkward farmers.* Indeed, many country dwellers welcome the chance of a wave or chat as you pass by on their land.

There are some Forestry Commission 'permitted tracks' shown in these walks which means that walkers are allowed access over them but not as of right. The remainder of roads and paths used are all defined as public rights of way under present legislation and as shown on the definitive map of Shropshire. We cannot lawfully be prohibited from passing over these. Physically, of course, a farm dog, a bull or an irate landowner can prevent us. In those unlikely circumstances, rather than risk life, limb or increased blood pressure in argument, it is probably best if you leave by your most convenient route and report the matter to the County Council.

On certain stretches in these walks you will notice small plastic way-mark signs on gateposts and stiles depicting a silhouette of a buzzard in flight against a white background.

This denotes that you are on the 'Shropshire Way', a recreational footpath made by linking public rights of way, bridleways and lanes; the brain-child and creation of members of the Shropshire Group of the Ramblers' Association and other walking groups in the area in conjunction with Shropshire County Council. In all, the Shropshire Way covers 172 miles; the main section of which is a loop of 125 miles from Wem in the North to Ludlow in the South.

WHAT TO TAKE TO WEAR This is a matter of personal taste and comfort. As none of the rambles or walks in this book are particularly arduous, strong shoes or boots and adequate waterproof clothing is all that you should need. In any season other than a good summer, it is probably best to take a spare sweater and if the walk is longer than a couple of hours, you may feel like packing a thermos and sandwiches in a small day pack. The important thing to remember is to try at all times to keep dry. If you become wet and have to stop for any reason such as a twisted ankle, even on this County's generally benign hills, you could put yourself at risk of hyperthermia, particularly if you are unaccompanied and there is no one to go for help.
There is no need to buy expensive boots and the good old welly is often one of the best bets for footwear except on the longer walks of three hours or more.

GRADES AND TIMES None of the walks in this book are arduous; most are moderate and some are easy. The definition of these words is a matter of personal interpretation but they should be well within the capabilities of the average healthy person. The times shown are based on an average pace of two miles per hour. This is not as slow as it seems because whilst your pace may naturally be quicker, you will be slowed up by stiles and gates and other obstructions not to mention ascent!

WHAT TO WATCH OUT FOR Each walk has points of interest, both natural and man-made, which might appeal. As will be obvious, I am neither a naturalist nor an ornithologist and therefore I have not detailed the many different species of wildlife to be found in the area although I have mentioned those most commonly seen including buzzards, kestrels, larks and wheatears, etc. The bird-watcher and botanist will find endless pleasure in discovering what the Shropshire Hills have to offer. (I have been told that a pair of Peregrine Falcons were seen on the Long Mynd in 1988!).

It is hoped that this book will show Shropshire as the superb county for walking that it is and introduce to those unfamiliar with the area the many attractive hills, particularly in the South of the county. Few of the hills are remote or very high; just remote and high enough to give a feeling of space and peace and perhaps to induce in the reader a liking - or even - an addiction for hill walking.

These hills cannot be said to be mountains. Indeed, the highest - Brown Clee - is under 2,000 ft in height, but their steepness is deceptive. They also have the beauty of variety. Stand on Stiperstones on a windswept January day and compare that ridge with the gentler uplands of the Clun Forest or with the wide expanse of the Longmynd and you will realise just how varied they are.

Hill-walking is many things to many people. To some it is a challenge; to some merely a chance to be in high places alone and away from the demands and responsibilities of daily life. For others it is to share the hills with friends in companionship and laughter or perhaps the chance to heal some wound inflicted by lowland life, circumstances or people. To me, it is something of all these and now is such an addiction as almost to be the reason for living. If when you have sampled some of these walks, you aspire to greater heights, then I hope you will look back on this border county with fondness.

To me, Shropshire is not yet a land of 'lost' content, more a place of 'found' contentment. I hope that will be so for you too and that you will come again to her 'happy highways'. I commend the hills of Shropshire to you!

FOLLOW THE COUNTRY CODE

Guard against all risks of fire
Fasten all gates
Keep dogs under proper control
Keep to paths across farmland
Leave no litter
Safeguard water supplies
Protect wildlife, wild plants and trees
Go carefully on country roads
Respect the life of the countryside

Remember also that if you have a choice between stile and gate always use the stile.

If you have to unfasten a gate, please secure it as you found it.

If you have to climb a gate, do so at the hinge-end and then one person at a time.

KEY

	CG	CATTLE GRID
	G	GATE
	S	STILE
	FB	FOOTBRIDGE
	▲	TRIGULATION POINT (USUALLY CONCRETE PILLARS ERECTED BY ORDNANCE SURVEYORS)
	H	HURDLE
	TP	TELEPHONE BOX
	WG	WICKET GATE
	KG	KISSING GATE
		METALLED ROAD
		UNMADE TRACK
- - - - -		PATH OR WAY (OFTEN UNDEFINED ON THE GROUND)
	LH	LEFT HAND
	RH	RIGHT HAND
	L	LEFT
	R	RIGHT
		MAST OR PYLON

Meaning	Symbol
SPRING	
STREAM	
HEIGHT IN METRES	•394
HEIGHT IN FEET	(1293)
TUMULUS	
ROCK OR ROCKY OUTCRO	
NATIONAL TRUST	N.T
FORESTRY COMMISSION	F.C
CAIRN	
WOODEN SIGNPOST	
RAILWAY	
MARSHY	
HEDGE	
CHAPEL	+
CHURCH	
BRIDGE	)(
TELEGRAPH POLES	o o o
OFFA'S DYKE WAY	O.DW

TOP OF PAGE IS NORTH

SKETCH MAPS ARE NOT DRAWN TO SCALE.

A. THE LONG MYND AND CHURCH STRETTON AREA

With hills such as the Long Mynd itself, the Lawley, Caer Caradoc, Ragleth, Hazler and Helmeth, to many this area *is* Shropshire's highlands. However, when all the other hills in this book have been walked, you may well feel differently.

Such well walked parts as the Cardingmill Valley are purposely omitted but other 'stars' are included, like Caer Caradoc. At least three of the walks take one onto the Long Mynd, a high, wide expanse worthy of great note and deserving ascent from different points.

In geological terms, the hills comprise two main groups running in a SE - NW direction, the eastern side of which includes, Caradoc and The Lawley and is composed of pre-Cambrian volcanic lavas and ashes. The area is dissected by a great fault in the earth's crust wherein now lie Church Stretton, Little Stretton and All Stretton. To the west is the barer but massive expanse of the Long Mynd - a smooth topped plateau cut on its eastern flanks by deep V-shaped, stream filled valleys known locally as 'batches' or 'hollows'. This is also pre-Cambrian but because the rocks are softer than those to the east of the fault, the Long Mynd looks smoother. The hills would have protruded above the glaciers of the Ice Age and although there is some evidence in the Marches that mankind was here as long ago as 12,000 B.C., the first substantial traces date from between 4,000 to 3,000 B.C. and it was during the Bronze Age that Man's hand really showed, being particularly obvious in the round barrows and low burial mounds to be found in so many places alongside the ancient track which runs atop the Long Mynd - the Portway. This well defined track runs along the complete length of the Long Mynd. It was first used by Neolithic axe-traders and was still recognised as a King's Highway as late as the Middle Ages. It is still a Queen's Highway as for the most part it is now a defined public right of way.

The town of Church Stretton draws many people for their retirement and certainly, it has the feel of a resort set amid glorious hill scenery. Mary Webb spent her honeymoon here and refers to it in her novels as Shepwardine. There are very few ancient buildings in the town, the finest older houses to be found in small All Stretton to the North and in beautiful Little Stretton to the South. Further South yet, is idyllic Minton which dates from Saxon times. As a centre for a holiday, Church Stretton offers a good rail service, hotels and numerous good guesthouses and restaurants.

A paradise for walkers, the area also absorbs others with such outdoor pursuits as horse-riding, golf, cycling, gliding and unfortunately motor cycling.

Whilst the Long Mynd is not Shropshire's highest hill, it is certainly its largest in terms of acreage and is not to be trifled with in bad weather despite its seeming lack of stature in comparison with other hills and mountains. To all intents and purposes it is a mountain; even the name is derived from the Cymraeg 'mynydd' meaning 'mountain' in English. As proof of how treacherous the hill can be, a tale to chill is that of the Rev. D. Carr who in 1865 nearly perished on the Long Mynd in a snowstorm and whose adventure is recorded in a little book which is still obtainable called 'A Night in the Snow'. Happily, he survived the ordeal but only just. 1865 or 1989, the hills and their weather can be lethal. Merely because they are under 2,000 feet high and they are not in Wales or Scotland, do not treat them lightly but give them the respect they deserve. That said, these hills can offer many hours of blissful, safe walking giving peace, solitude and a beauty of a kind rarely to be found in England.

A1 Plowden-The Long Mynd-Churchmoor Hill-Plowden

Start & Finish: The Old Post Office, Plowden
Grid Ref. SO 382876
Approx. Distance: 5-6 miles
Approx. Time: 2½-3 hours
Grade: Moderate – can be muddy on some tracks.
Pub/Café availability: Little – nearest are The Crown at Wentnor & The Ragleth Arms and The Green Dragon at Little Stretton.
What to Watch out for: Buzzards. The Portway (see Introduction to this section). In Summer – Whinberries, Wheatears, Pippets, Larks.

1. From the Old Post Office at Plowden, follow metalled lane North and head away from the main road for about ¼ mile. In early Summer look out for masses of red campions, blue vetches and forget-me-knots in the hedgerow. If blessed with a clear day, as you gently climb, glance L to the rising, wind-blown line of beeches fringing Linley Hill and a few miles away to the bulwarks of Corndon Hill behind.

2. Over the CG, turn sharp R through a gate. You have now almost doubled-back in direction. (Watch out for the 'Buzzard' waymark denoting that you are on The Shropshire Way. This should be attached to the CG post). You are now on a track which climbs and winds gently as you ascend. Pausing for breath, glance back over the valley. The delightful River Onny winds its way through the tree-filled valley. During the main glaciation period, most of this region was invaded by streams of ice fed from the mountains of Wales. The course you are now looking at was probably made when water from melting ice occupying the broad valley to the North-West grew in volume and rushed to find an outlet South of the Long Mynd. On a Spring or Summer day here the 'Glacial Retreat Phenomena' strains the imagination a little, though perhaps not on a typical Shropshire February day.

3. Still climbing, you pass through two more gates. After the second (and sheep fold), the track forks. Bear R and continue up, now contouring the hill. The views westwards become obscured by the ridge above you but eastwards – to your R – can be seen the distant Black Mountains of Wales like a long, flat table-top and nearer, the 'high-browed Clee' (Titterstone) and the tops of Brown Clee.

4. The track peters out for a while, but follow the same line upwards, pass through another gate and across another field.

5. At the next fence, take the right-hand of the two gates and, keeping the fence on your L, continue your line. Soon, a conifer plantation outline appears on the horizon ahead of you.

A1

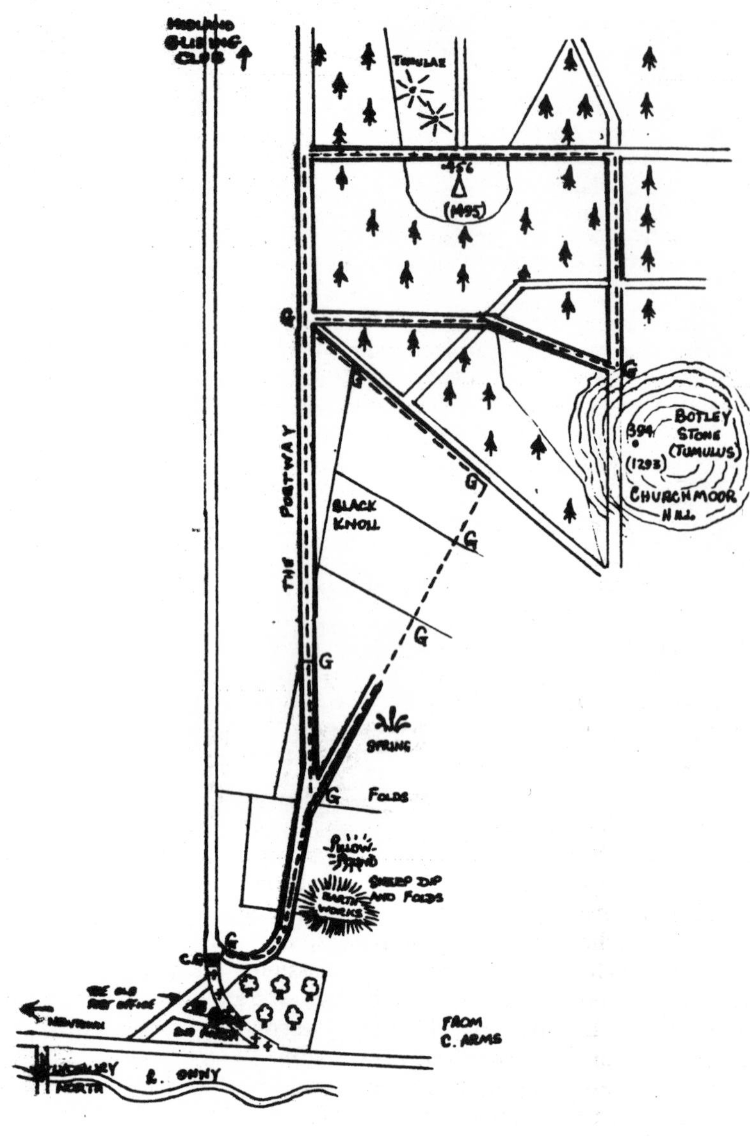
456
(1495)
THE PORTWAY
G
BLACK KNOLL
394
BOTLEY STONE (TUMULUS)
(1293)
CHURCHMOOR HILL
SPRING
FOLDS
SHEEP DIP AND FOLDS
EARTH WORKS
C.G.
FROM C. ARMS
R. ONNY

6. At the edge of plantation, go through another gate. Keeping the fence of the forest on your R, bear slightly L and follow forestry boundary to the end where you join a wide grassy track on the top of the Long Mynd ridge. This is The Portway, a pre-historic road which runs atop the Long Mynd for its length. We shall meet it again later but for now, leave it immediately passing through a gate and sharp R into the plantation where the track becomes grassy and delightful to tread. It is wide enough not to allow the forestry on either side to become too oppressive.

7. At a Forestry Commission 'hard' track, cross over and continue along the grassy 'ride' . Do not deviate at all but follow this until the edge of the woodland is reached.

8. Continue, keeping the fence on your R. On a clear day there are good distant views ahead and to your R. Ahead, on a grassy knoll is the summit of Churchmoor Hill.

9. Still on your path, one can now either go through the gate in the fence and picnic on the hill top or, if weather or inclination does not permit, keep in the cover of the trees and still enjoy the views South and Eastwards. (You have now reached about halfway on the walk).

10. Refreshed, if only by the views, turn L and take the track (often muddy) upwards through the trees (North).

11. At the first 'crossroads', the muddy track joins a hard FC track coming in from your L. Join this track and continue in the same direction you have been walking.

12. At the next junction, turn L: soon, you will come into a heather-clad clearing. To your R (North) is the open Long Mynd plateau. L (South) a few yards away you will see the concrete trig. post poking above the heather. If clear far, far away are the Black Mountains again. Ahead of you, as you start to descend the now grassy track (your climbing is over) your breath will be taken away now not by effort but by the views through the trees. If you are lucky, you will see the Berwyns of North Wales. If you can draw your gaze away for a moment, you will notice on your immediate right, two small Bronze-age tumuli.

13. When you reach the edge of the forestry, you join again the Portway, a little further North from where you left it earlier. Turn L along the old track and continue along this, the trees on your L, the wonderful views on your R, until you reach the gate where you joined and quickly left the Portway at 6 above.

14. Continue through the gate and keep to the high track rolling gently ahead of you between the heather. You will possibly spot a buzzard and in Spring and Summer, almost certainly, you will hear and see larks and pippits. If very good weather (and this is possible

even in January and February) on the horizon to your right, you will be able to see massive Cader Idris. The heather will give way to a golden carpet of whinberry shrubs as you traverse Black Knoll. Then, simply follow the track downhill to a gate. Go through this, keep in the same direction of descent and you will reach the track again near the sheepfolds that you left at 3 above.

15. Re-trace your steps to Plowden. If you have been lucky enough to cover this last stretch of descent towards the end of a sunny day, the silhouette of the hills and the shining, gold Onny below will make this unforgettable. This descent to Plowden is one of my favourite walks.

A2 All Stretton-Betchcott Hill-Bridges-All Stretton

Start & Finish: NT car park, All Stretton
Grid Ref. SO 456955
Approx. Distance: 11-12 miles
Approx. Time: 5-6 hours
Pub/Café availability: The Horseshoe Inn — Bridges. Yew Tree Inn — All Stretton. Teas at farm near Ratlinghope Church.
Grade: Fairly strenuous in parts but good tracks and paths.
What to watch out for: Bluebells en masse shortly after the start on the slopes (L). Cranesbill in hedgerows of lane down to All Stretton near end. Marsh marigold alongside Darnford Brook and violets and wood sorrel in Darnford area. Trefoil and masses of gorse in Golden Valley. Buzzards (particularly in Golden Valley), larks, pippits and dippers along Jonathan's Hollow. Campion, vetches and foxgloves galore in hedgerows. Ratlinghope Church with old oak door dated 1625. Wrought iron altar rails and chancel panelling of Georgian period. The ancient yew tree on W side of church had a girth of over 17 ft. in 1984. Great oval pre-historic camp on Ratlinghope Hill described by Mary Webb in 'Golden Arrow'.

1. From NT car park at All Stretton, take the track into the hills: this diminishes into a path.

2. After crossing two FB's, keeping the stream on your L climb steadily — though not too steeply (yet!) for about three quarters of a mile.

3. As the path runs deeper into Jonathan's Hollow, keep a look out for a solitary Hawthorn tree on your R. (There are not many on your R, although they are numerous on the slopes across the stream to your L). At about the same time as the tree comes into view, ahead and above, you will see a jagged tooth of rock poking out of the hill slope: this is Jonathan's Rock.

4. Just before reaching the tree, turn R onto a narrow stony track that zig- zags steeply up the hillside.

A2

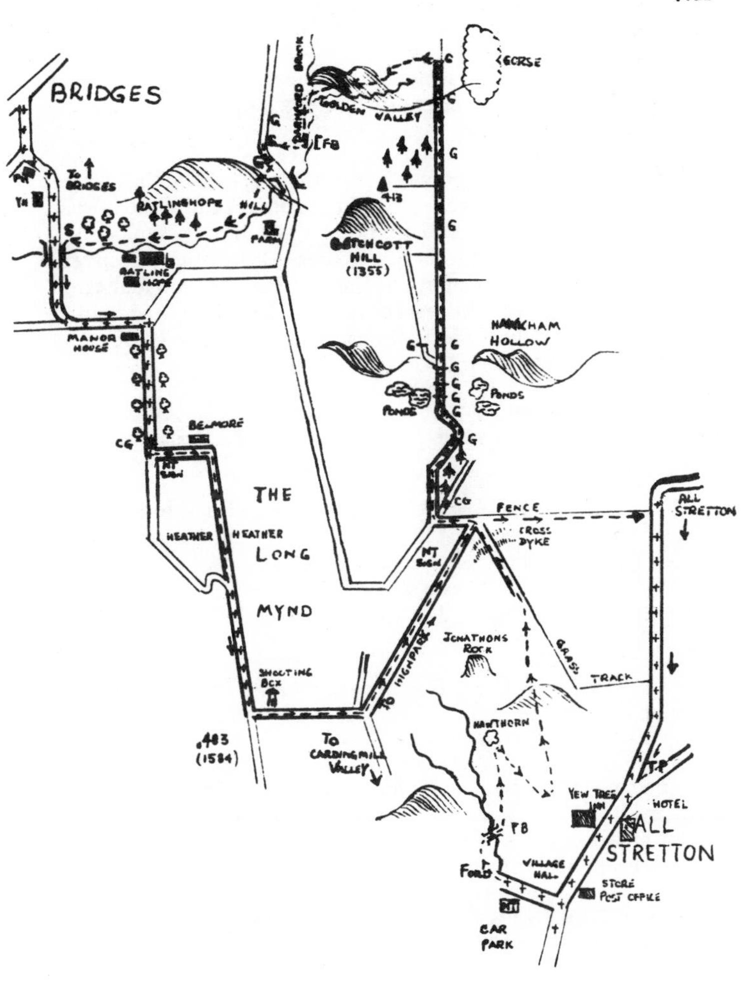
BRIDGES
YH
To BRIDGES
RATLINGHOPE HILL
FARM
RATLING HOPE
MANOR HOUSE
GORSE
GOLDEN VALLEY
FB
413
(1355)
PONDS
PONDS
BELMORE
NT SIGN
THE LONG MYND
HEATHER
HEATHER
NT SIGN
FENCE
CROSS DYKE
ALL STRETTON
JONATHONS ROCK
GRASS TRACK
SHOOTING BOX
TO HIGHPARK
483
(1584)
To CARDINGMILL VALLEY
HAWTHORN
YEW TREE INN
HOTEL
T.P.
ALL STRETTON
FB
FORD
VILLAGE HALL
STORE
POST OFFICE
CAR PARK

5. At the top, bear slightly R until you reach a broad grassy track rising gently. Follow this, now bearing L, crossing an ancient grass-covered ditch (Cross Dyke). You begin to walk parallel to a fence on your R. Keep this so until the fence joins a tarmac road and a CG on your R. You will see a NT sign on your L.

6. Cross road and keep in same direction, now on a stony track. (You are on the Portway — the ancient Long Mynd track — and you remain on this for some time).

7. Enjoy wide views R over North Shropshire plain, and the bump of the Wrekin. After a short while, many miles distant and ahead of you, the Berwyns of North Wales come into view and as you continue, slightly nearer and to your L the Stiperstones toothy ridge will appear and then Corndon Hill, assuming a clear day. Pass through four gates: the fifth is one of a pair. The most obvious track seems to lead from the L gate. DO NOT TAKE THIS. Instead, go through the R gate and keep the fence now on your L.

8. After the next gate, to your L and quite nearby in a field you will see the concrete pillar of a trig. point some 4ft. high. This is Betchcott Hill.

9. The track dips and rises slightly and improves from stony to part-metalled. At the 2nd gate past the trig. point, you enter a gorse-lined section. Here, leave the track and pass through a gate, L. Below you lies Golden Valley — aptly named when gorse is in full bloom. There is no well-defined path but head downhill, keeping the bed of the gully on your L.

10. You pass by two lovely Beech trees on your L. Keep in same direction — brook on your L — across a meadow and over a stile in a fence.

11. You will notice another, larger stream now on your R: this is Darnford Brook. Walk on down the hill, between streams. You find you are on a little grassy ridge between them. At end of ridge, turn R and below you, there should be seen a small wooden FB (it IS small).

12. After crossing this, ahead you will see a stile next to a gate under some large Oaks. Cross stile and on the track, turn L.

13. After a few yards and before you reach the ford to Lower Darnford Farm, turn R and pass through a gate. Darnford Brook is on your L and you follow this delightful stretch of water until you reach the stile at the Bridges road. This section is quite long, intercepted with stiles. The cattle and sheep graze peacefully together, the brook sings along to you. On your R rises Ratlinghope Hill, on your L the lovely valley and the flanks of the Long Mynd. You pass by the hamlet of Ratlinghope (pronounced locally as 'Ratchup') and identified in Mary Webb's novels as 'Slepe'. If you have time, leave your path for a while at the FB on your L and explore the church.

14. Eventually, you come to the end of this idyllic section when you reach the stile at the lane. If you turn R along the lane and take the first L, you come to Bridges, called a 'little Venice' where the bubbling waters of Darnford Brook and River East Onny converge. The pub makes a welcome stop and by the time you reach here you will probably have been walking some 2½-3 hours and feel in need of sustenance.

15. Returning to the stile at the road, continue on over the small stone bridge (not as ancient as it looks) or, if you have not diverted to Bridges at all, at that stile, you simply turn L and over the small stone bridge.

16. Follow lane, turning L at first junction. Pass Manor House on your R and take first turning R up lane heading away from the valley and passing between rows of Beeches. This is rather a climb. Pause from time to time for breath and look down onto the valley you have just walked and the hamlet of Ratlinghope nestling below.

17. At top of hill cross CG and immediately turn L up a track towards Belmore Farm. (Ignore signs discouraging this). At entrance to Belmore's garden keep to track and bear R keeping their fence on your L.

18. Head straight up hill without deviating L or R. You climb steadily through heather.

19. After half a mile you will meet the tarmac road at a bend. Bear L onto road and keep to this until you reach the shooting-box (in the shape of a large ridge tent) which appears on your L.

20. You will see a deep, peaty track to your L. Take this, passing by the shooting box now with this still on your L.

21. Simply follow this wide, dark track through the heather and along the top of the Long Mynd plateau for about half a mile. You will then see this forks and notice a wooden post marked 'Cardingmill' in one direction; 'Highpark' in another. Take the Highpark track; i.e. you neither turn R down to Cardingmill nor fork L but keep in the same direction along the top.

22. Soon, as you descend slightly, you will see the fence you left earlier at No. 5. On reaching this, turn R and descend the broad grassy track downhill, keeping fence on your L, until you reach a tarmac lane and sign post for All Stretton.

23. Follow the All Stretton sign and keep to this lane until you reach the road junction in the village with the phone box on your L. Turn R along road and take first R after Yew Tree Inn. After a third of a mile you should reach the Car Park again. One last look around you and behind looms Caradoc seeming to rise sheerly and vertically — but that's for another day.

A3

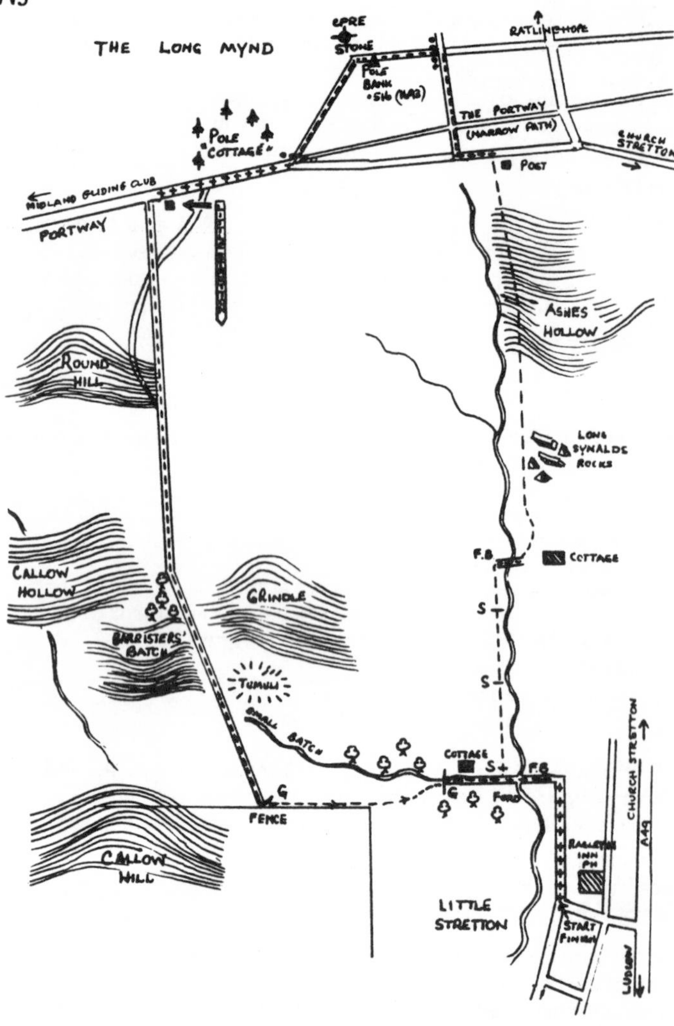
THE LONG MYND
STONE
POLE BANK
516 (NAG)
RATLINGHOPE
THE PORTWAY
(NARROW PATH)
CHURCH STRETTON
POST
POLE "COTTAGE"
MIDLAND GLIDING CLUB
PORTWAY
ASHES HOLLOW
ROUND HILL
LONG SYNALDS ROCKS
F.B
COTTAGE
S
CALLOW HOLLOW
GRINDLE
BARRISTERS' BATCH
TUMULI
SMALL BATCH
COTTAGE
F.B
G
FORD
FENCE
CALLOW HILL
INN
PH
CHURCH STRETTON
A49
LITTLE STRETTON
START

A3 Little Stretton-Ashes Hollow-Pole Bank-Round Hill-Callow Hill-Little Stretton

Start & Finish: Little Stretton.
Grid Ref. SO 442918
Approx. Distance: 5-6 miles
Approx. Time: 2½-3 hours
Pub/Café availability: Ragleth Inn & Green Dragon — Little Stretton
Grade: Moderate. Paths can be muddy.
What to watch out for: Curlew, pippits, wheatears, dippers. Tumuli on Grindle Hill. Scenic Direction Stone ('toposcope') on Pole Bank erected by Shropshire Branch of Council for the Protection of Rural England to mark its Jubilee in 1986.

1. From Ragleth Inn, take lane alongside and bear R at brook. Follow lane to ford and FB. Cross FB and immediately cross stile on your R. Cross field (often occupied by campers) keeping the stream on your R.

2. Cross another stile and field.

3. At next FB cross water and continue into hills, the stream now on your L. This will remain so for some time.

4. Gradually the path becomes narrower and more rocky. Do not be discouraged but do be careful. The valley sides become more enclosing and steeper. Keep to path.

5. At the first meeting of streams, keep to that flowing L from the hills. The path becomes even more narrow but, with care, is not dangerous.

6. Eventually, the path enters a wider valley and becomes grassy. Follow this (it may mean crossing and re-crossing the water from time to time) and at the next meeting of valleys, keep to the R. The stream should now be on your L. Continue the gradual, steady ascent.

7. Presently, the path narrows and the stream becomes a trickle as you reach the head of the valley. Continue until you reach the metalled road and a wooden waymark post. Turn L and, after a few yards, R along a stony track through heather.

8. Ignore the first narrow paths which cross at right-angles. (This is part of the Portway across the Long Mynd). Pausing for breath, look back to distant Brown Clee and Titterstone — if your day is clear. If misty, press on and think of tea.

9. At next junction, turn L, passing between four wooden posts and in a few yards you reach the highest point on the Long Mynd — Pole Bank — and its trig. point. On a good day, the view is tremendous. Nearby you will see the 'toposcope' and plaque erected by CPRE.
A pleasant few minutes can be whiled away spotting The Arans, Cader Idris, the Brecon Beacons and the Black Mountains.

10. Leaving this high-spot, keep on path in same direction until you reach its end at four more wooden posts and the metalled road. Turn R along road, passing Pole Cottage on your R. This is not a cottage now but a corrugated iron shed surrounded by trees.

11. Continue for a few minutes along the road until you see another wooden way-mark post on your L. This directs you down to Little Stretton. Turn L off road and step lightly along the broad, peaty track through the heather. In Spring and Summer, you will more than likely hear the plaintive call of the curlew. Vast expanses of high moorland stretch around you making you feel more apart from 'civilisation' than actually you are.

12. When the track forks, you can either go L, in which case you will contour Round Hill or continue straight ahead over the top. If you go straight on; at top, bear slightly L downhill until you meet the main path again at Barrister's Plain.

13. Stay on path which begins to rise again and pass three Hawthorn trees on your R. Look down R into Barrister's Batch and Callow Hollow. This section is particularly lovely towards the end of a sunny day, when the water in Callow Hollow threads like a silver ribbon through the dark hills.

14. The path is now wholly grass and delightful underfoot as it contours Grindle Hill rising on your L. Here, break off a detour if you fancy a spot of steep climbing and take in Grindle Hill itself. You will be on the site of an ancient tumuli. Back to the path you left, follow this around the hillside and crossing the shoulder between Grindle and Callow Hill, turn (still on path) slightly R. You now descend on the flank of Callow as it rises on your R. On your L, far below, is bracken clad Small Batch and ahead lies Little Stretton below you.

15. The grass track meets a fence and gate. Do NOT pass through gate, but turn L, keeping fence on your R and descend the steep section into Small Batch. Take care here; the path is steep and slippery when wet.

16. At bottom, pass through gate — usually very muddy — skip over stream and passing cottage on your L, re-cross the FB you met earlier. Thence, R and back to the village and a choice of two good inns — if you have timed it properly!

A4 Minton Green-Callow Hollow-The Long Mynd-Minton Hill-Packetstone Hill-Minton Green

Start & Finish: Minton Green.
Grid Ref. SO 432908

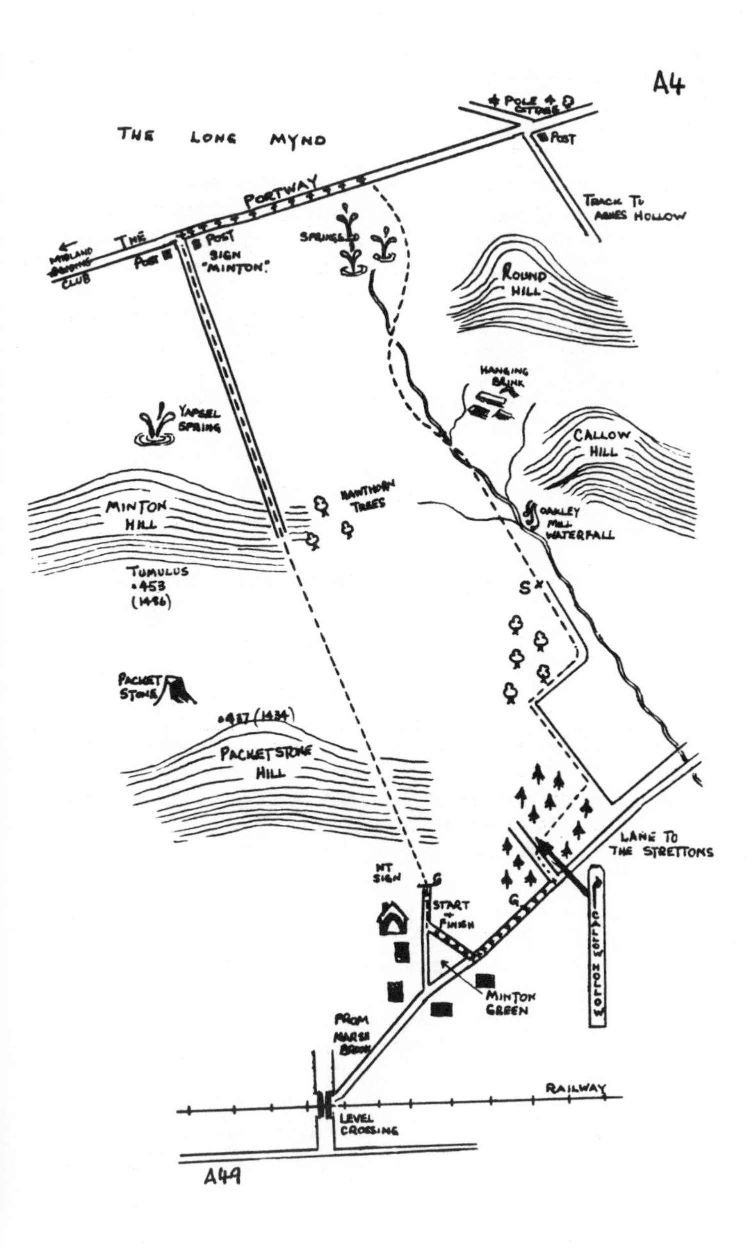

A4
POLE
POST
THE LONG MYND
THE PORTWAY
← MIDLAND
CLUB
POST
POST
SIGN "MINTON"
SPRINGS
TRACK TO ASHES HOLLOW
ROUND HILL
HANGING BRINK
YAPSEL SPRING
CALLOW HILL
HAWTHORN TREES
MINTON HILL
OAKLEY MILL WATERFALL
TUMULUS •453 (1486)
S
PACKET STONE
•437 (1434)
PACKETSTONE HILL
LANE TO THE STRETTONS
NT SIGN
G
START FINISH
G
CALLOW HOLLOW
MINTON GREEN
FROM MARSH BROOK
RAILWAY
LEVEL CROSSING
A49

Approx. Distance: 4-5 miles
Approx. Time: 2-2½ hours
Pub/Café availability: Nearest at Little Stretton one mile to North; The Ragleth Inn and The Green Dragon Inn.
Grade: Easy
What to watch out for: The moated Saxon Mound at Minton Green and cruck- framed timber cottage at Minton Green. Buzzards, larks, pippits, dippers (along Callow Brook). Foxgloves rampant in Callow Coppice.

1. From Minton Green, take lane northwards towards the Strettons. Descend lane steeply, passing a field gate on your L. At bottom of incline — about quarter of a mile from the start — turn L through a gap in the hedge and enter a small conifer plantation.

2. After 10 yards, turn R into the trees. Do not miss this turning: if unobscured by undergrowth, you may be assisted by a wooden way-mark post — 'Callow Hill'.

3. After a few more yards, you reach a fence. Turn L and keep to the narrow and often overgrown path; the fence will be on your R. In summer, this area is a mass of foxgloves. Also, after high winds, this path can be something of an obstacle course, but persevere.

4. Eventually, you leave the woodland at a stile. Over this, follow the path up and into the Hollow. You join the stream gurgling on your R.

5. Pause in a while to admire the small (but perfectly formed) Oakleymill Waterfall. In relation to Niagara, it is miniscule, but a lovely and pleasant diversion, nonetheless. Callow Hill rises sharply on the other side of the stream. Thankfully, its flanks are not on this itinery!

6. Pressing on, keep the stream on your R until the valley widens slightly. Here, you will find it easier if you cross the water but keep in the same direction upstream. Presently, an outcrop of rock will come into view. This is Hanging Rock and a good place for a rest and a look back into the batch.

7. Then, back to the other side of the stream and as the watercourse becomes narrower, bear R, rising into the heather-clad moorland of the Long Mynd.

8. Keep in the same direction and you should pass by a pool on your L. Proceed on, through the heather until you reach a metalled road. (If you come to a wider, peaty track, you have moved too far R but do not worry. In that case, simply turn L along the track and you will soon reach the road).

9. At road, turn L and enjoy the wide expanse of lonely moorland until you reach a wooden marker post on your L — 'Minton'. Turn L onto peaty wide track and do not leave this.

10. After some time, the track rises over Minton Hill and begins to descend slightly. You have the choice of going straight ahead over Packetstone Hill top or of keeping to the path after Minton Hill and bearing slightly L, passing a stand of Hawthorn trees on your L. Keep in same general direction and gradually, the descent steepens and the hamlet of Minton will come into view. Head for this; the track ever more steep until you reach a gate and the NT sign for Minton.

11. Pass through gate and follow track — after a few yards, turning R along it through barns and cottages until you reach the Green once more. Note the fine example of a cruck-framed house on your R in this tiny lane. The descent to Minton illuminates well the formation of this well-preserved typically Saxon village — an especial joy in early Spring when the village green itself is asway with daffodils.:

A5 Hope Bowdler Hill

Start & Finish: Hope Bowdler village.
Grid Ref. SO 475925
Approx. Distance: 4 miles
Approx. Time: 2 hours
Grade: Easy. Good paths with very little ascent
Pub/Café availability: Many in Church Stretton — 2 miles NW.
What to watch out for: Buzzards and kestrels in particular. Hope Bowdler Church. This stands in the delightful village which nestles in the hills. The church is 19th C. but built in the 13th C. style and is approached by a splendid avenue of Irish yews. The pulpit is 300 years old; the bell dates from medieval times.
N.B. *This walk can be linked with A6 and/or A7, making a total of 9 miles if only taken in with A6 and a good day's walk of 14 miles if also added to A7. For the link-up, at WG (10 below), keep straight on with the hillock on your L. Cross a short boggy section passing between bracken and crossing over a ditch/stream. Pass by a small plantation on your R and enter track at A on the Sketch for walk A6.*

1. From the village centre, take the main road towards Much Wenlock and take the stile by the entrance to Upper House to enter a stony, rising track. (Upper House is on your R as you walk the track).

2. The track continues to the R of a barn BUT you take the stile which is on the L of the barn and, almost immediately, take another stile after passing the barn.

3. You now enter a 'green lane' with a stream a few yards below you on your L. Keep to this lane and pass over another stile next to a gate.

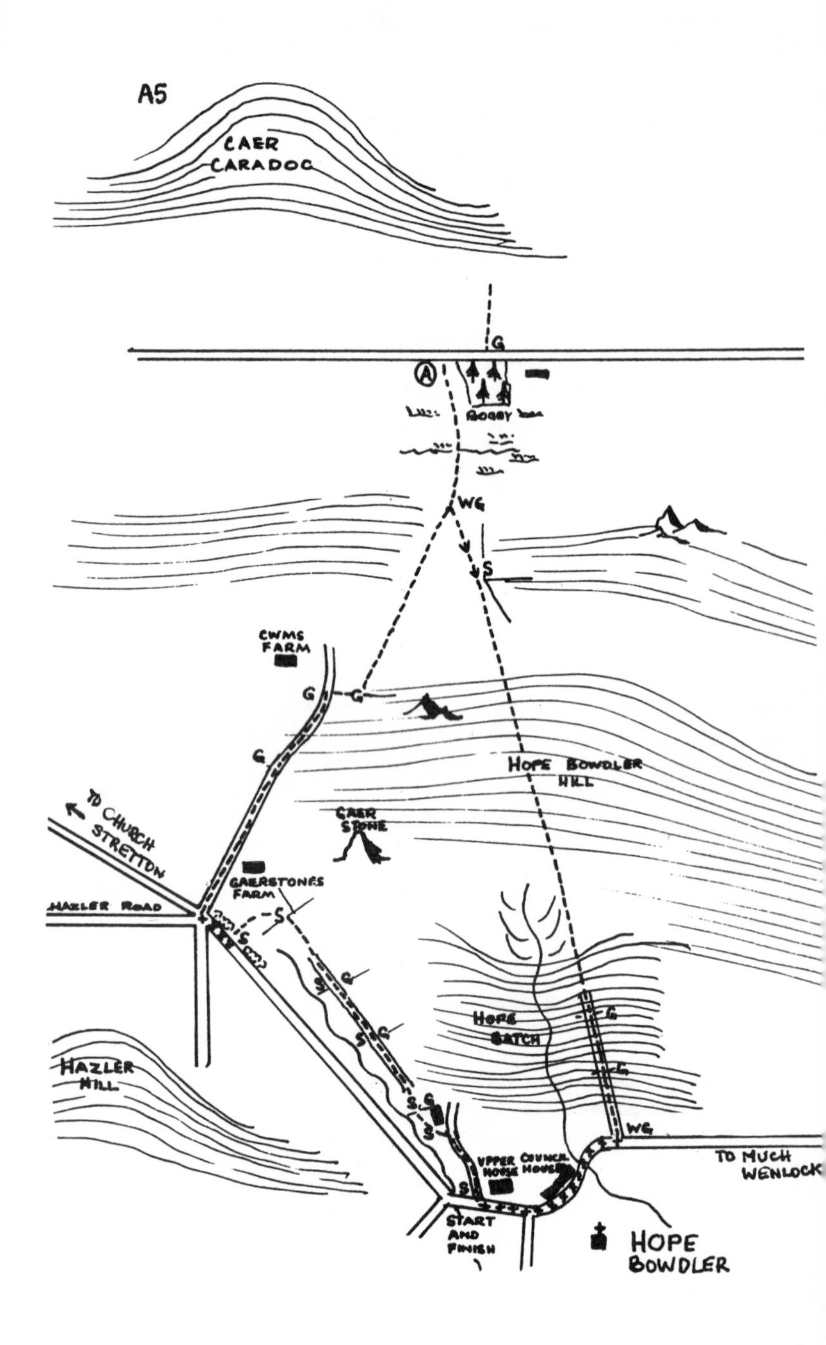
A5
CAER CARADOC
G
A
BOGGY
WG
S
CWMS FARM
G
G
G
HOPE BOWDLER HILL
TO CHURCH STRETTON
CAER STONE
CAERSTONES FARM
HAZLER ROAD
S
S
G
G
S
HOPE BATCH
G
G
HAZLER HILL
S
S
WG
TO MUCH WENLOCK
UPPER HOUSE
COUNCIL HOUSE
S
START AND FINISH
HOPE BOWDLER

4. You now enter a field with a hillside on your R and the stream still below you on your L. Across the field, take another stile which is next to a gate.

5. Keep to the same level and direction, contouring the hillside, quite low. Above you on your R rears Black Planting Rock and across the valley to your L you will see masted, green Hazler Hill.

6. Cross field and take in another stile. Pass to R of a telegraph pole in the next field and veer slightly to the L and downhill to enter the road by a stile in a hedge.

7. On road, turn R and after a few yards, take the first track on your R; the entrance to Gaer Stones Farm.

8. The track rises, passing between the farm buildings and becomes stonier. Pass through a gate and keep to the track as it bears R and slightly uphill. From here, you will have excellent views of the whole extent of Caer Caradoc on your L and ahead of you.

9. Pass through another gate and then towards a ruined cottage (Cwms Farm) on your L. By the cottage, take a gate in the fence on your R. (There may be a helpful sign — 'Footpath is that way'! and an arrow).

10. Through gate, turn L and follow the path on the lower slopes of Hope Bowdler Hill. High above you on your R is Gaerstone Rock while away to your L between the folds of the hills, lies Church Stretton with the Long Mynd staunch beyond.

11. You reach a single WG: do NOT go through this, but turn R and up the hill through the bracken quite steeply. You will reach a col or saddle and on your left in a fence you will see a stile. Do not take this, but pass by with it on your L and keep bearing slightly R along a grassy path and which skirts the highest part of the hill over which — unfortunately — there is no public footpath. Keep to the grassy track with a lower hill on your L, following this way in a southerly direction. The views from here are wide to your L over Wenlock Edge and beyond to Brown Clee and Titterstone.

12. Soon — too soon — you start to descend and find yourself walking alongside a small valley on your R — Hope Batch — and halfway along this, you will pass through a gate and enter a grassy, descending track. The hill you can see ahead of you and slightly to your R is Ragleth Hill.

13. You reach the Much Wenlock — Church Stretton road by a single gate, turn R by some council houses and return to your start.

A6

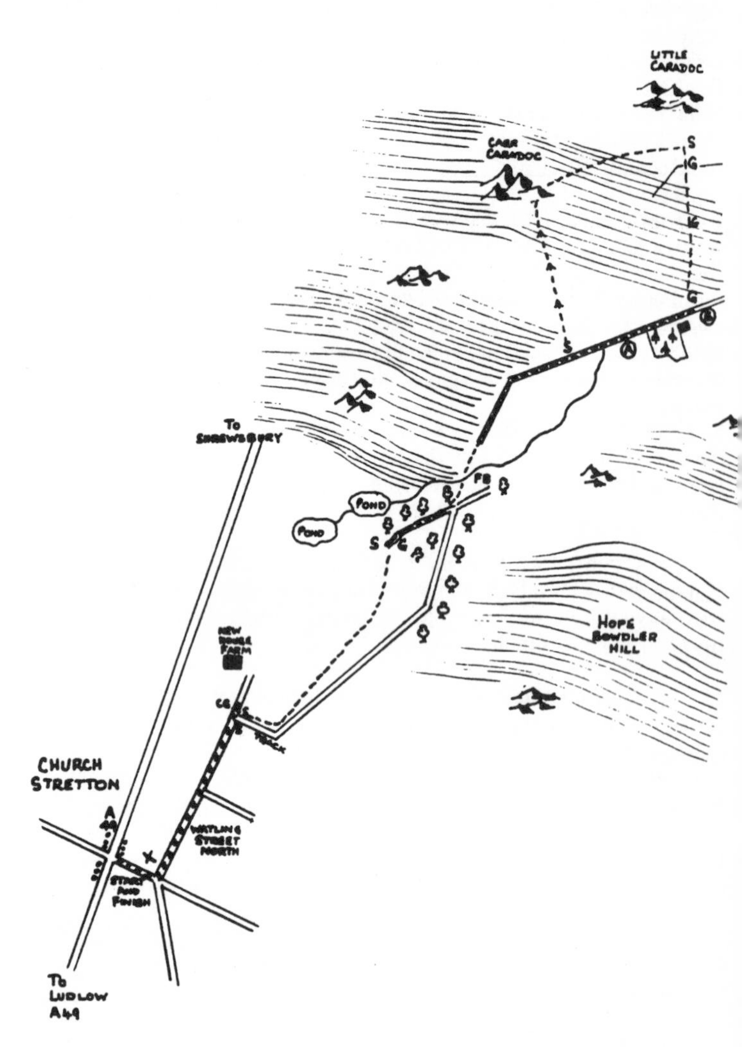

LITTLE CARADOC
CAER CARADOC
To
POND
POND
FB
HOPE BOWDLER HILL
CHURCH STRETTON
A 49
WATLING STREET NORTH
TRACK
To LUDLOW A49

A6 Caer Caradoc

Start & Finish: Traffic lights on A49 at Church Stretton.
Grid Ref. SO 456936
Approx. Distance: 5 miles
Approx. Time: 2½ hours.
Grade: Moderate. Steep ascents and descents. Good tracks and paths.
Pub/Café availability: Many at Church Stretton.
What to watch out for: Kestrels, ravens and buzzards in particular. Caer Caradoc fort; possibly the site of Caradoc's (Caractacus's) last stand against the Romans. (See also Caer Caradoc note for Walk D3). Enclosing some six acres; this long, oval camp dates from pre-history and rises sharply to 1,505 feet. It is outstanding (in every sense of the word) among Church Stretton's hills not only for its height and steepness but also for its bold appearance from below. The rocks forming the hill and cropping out at picturesque angles are volcanic in origin and are of the pre-Cambrian period; i.e. the oldest rock to be found in the County. The ditch of the ramparts is obvious and that, together with the rocky outcrops, afford good shelter for walker and sheep alike.
N.B. *This can be linked to walks A5 and A7. For A5, take in the note at the head of that walk. For A7 continue N over Little Caradoc at No. 8 below and take in the 'link-up' directions at head of A7 to join the start of that walk at Comley. (B on the sketch for A7).*

1. From Church Stretton traffic lights, take the Much Wenlock road (Sandford Avenue) and after a few yards, take first turning L to enter Watling Street North, passing by the Catholic Church on your L near the junction.

2. Keep to this lane and where Helmeth Road turns R, you keep straight on as the lane narrows. As you round the next bend, Caer Caradoc rises high above you ahead.

3. Where the lane ends at a CG at the entrance to a farm, do not take the first stile on your R, but take the second, i.e. that to the R of the CG itself and skirt the field, keeping the hedge/fence on your R but following its line.

4. At the next gate and stile together, cross stile and passing some fishponds on your L, keep on along the muddy track passing through trees and with a stream on your L.

5. After 50 yards, keep a look out for a narrow path leading off on your L. Take this and cross a FB over the stream. Keep to the path on the other side as it rises and broadens and as you begin to skirt the lower flanks of Caradoc on your L.

6. When you reach a stile in the fence on your L, take this and ascend the hill — steeply — but on a well-defined path worn by the weary feet

of the many who have trodden here before you and, you will be surprised to hear, have survived!

7. The highest point is marked by a stone cairn. You will be at 459 m (1,505 ft) and 360 degrees will reveal splendid views of the mountains of North, Mid and South Wales, the Shropshire Plain and East over Wenlock Edge, the Clees to the distant Clent Hills in the West Midlands. Church Stretton and its attendant villages are snug below you and the batches and hollows of the eastern flank of the vast Long Mynd are especially clear. The ravens, buzzards and, in particular, the kestrels abound. (I once counted 11 kestrels and this number is quite a regular feature).

8. Refreshed either by food or by the views (or both) stay in a northerly direction — i.e. towards the spine of The Lawley — and descend to a stile. (Here, you may decide to lengthen your day by continuing on to The Lawley. If so, see 'link-up' note at head of Walk A7).

9. If returning to your start, near the stile which is halfway down Caer Caradoc, you will see a gate in a fence on your R, take this and enter a high pasture. In this, contour the side of Caradoc, keeping the fence and top of the hill on your R.

10. Pass through the next gate and gradually bear R across another field — a high plateau which eventually descends to a gate to join the track at B in the sketch. (Here, you can re-join the Walk A5 directions if you have linked this to Walk A5 in order to return to Hope Bowdler). Otherwise, turn R when through the gate and continue along the track until you are able to re-trace your steps from No. 6 and return to your start at Church Stretton.

Caer Caradoc from the Lawley summit (A6 & A7)

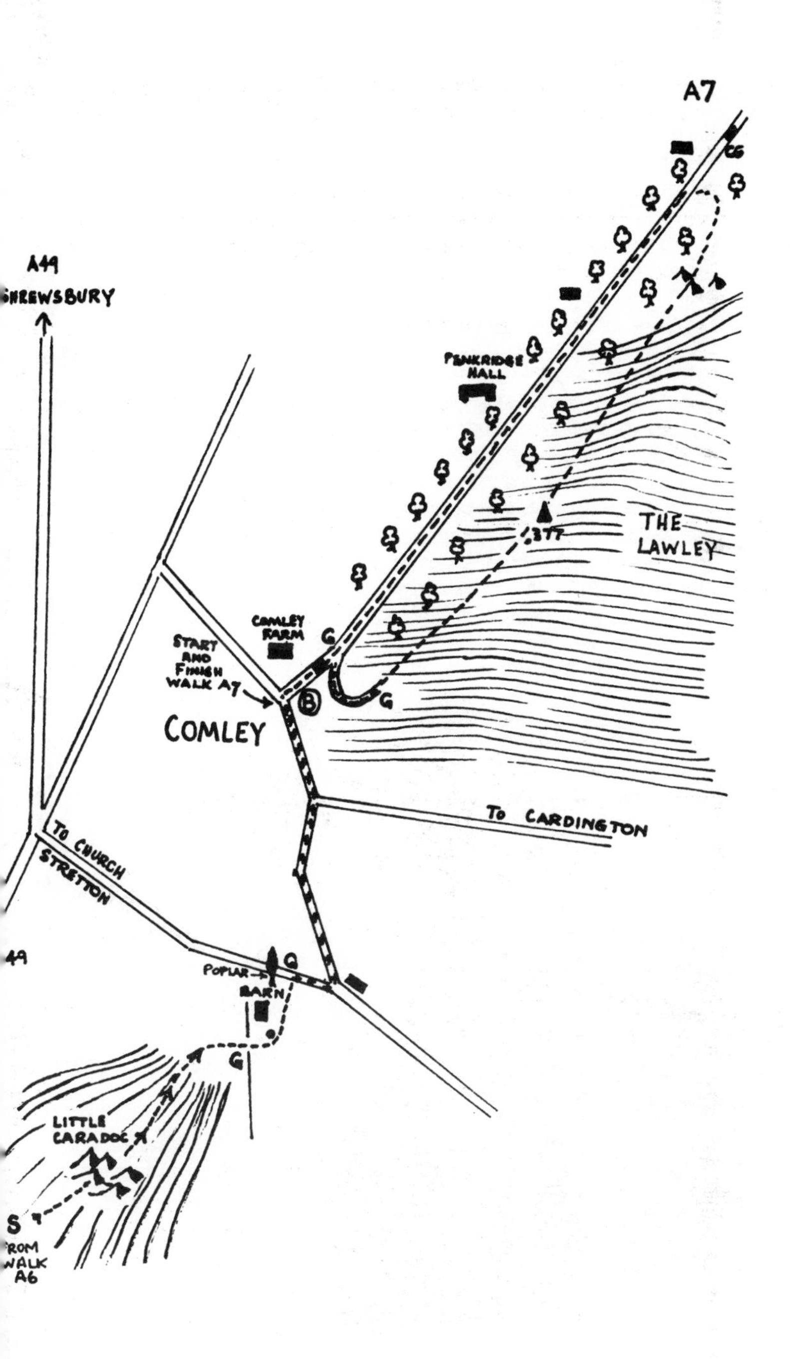
A7
CG
A49
SHREWSBURY
PENKRIDGE HALL
THE LAWLEY
377
COMLEY FARM
G
START AND FINISH WALK A7
B
COMLEY
TO CARDINGTON
TO CHURCH STRETTON
POPLAR
BARN
LITTLE CARADOC
FROM WALK A6

A7 The Lawley

Start & Finish: Comley.
Grid Ref: SO 485968
Approx. Distance: 5 miles
Approx. Time: 2½ hours
Grade: Moderate. Good paths and tracks with some steepness. A fine ridge walk.
Pub/Café availability: Many at Church Stretton. 3 miles SW 'Little Chef' at Leebotwood on A49.
What to watch out for: Buzzards, kestrels and ravens. Masts: the twin poles of weathered wood atop the summit are taken down and burnt whenever an heir of the Lord of the Manor reaches 21 to then be replaced with newer wood — at least, so local legend provides!
N.B. *For 'link-up' from Walk A6, over stile at No. 8 on A6 (Point A on A7 sketch) continue descending over the top of Little Caradoc until at the end of a very steep descent, where you turn R and after a few yards, take a gate in a fence on your L to enter a field. (Immediately on entering the field you should see a small barn on your L). Cross field, bearing L to reach a gate with a Poplar tree on its L. Cross gate to enter lane. The lane winds and at the first junction, bear L. At next junction, bear L also and take the first track on your R — the entrance to Comley Farm — and join directions for A7 below. (B on A7 sketch).*

1. From lane at the entrance to Comley Farm, take the track, passing over a CG on your way. Follow track round a RH bend and a sharp LH bend and then turn L, leaving the track and head up the hill after passing through a gate at the start. The southern end of The Lawley's ridge rises before you.

2. Simply climb! The way is quite steep, but you are rewarded by the views. At the highest point 377 m (1,236 ft) — you will come to a trig point next to which are two rough-hewn wooden posts some twelve feet or more in height. (See note at head of this walk).

3. Keep in same direction and gradually descend until you reach the foot of the ridge at its northern end. Here, where the paths part, you turn L and in a short while will join a track which comes in from your R. You are now also in a small wooded section.

4. Follow this track all the way to a gate, on your way enjoying the views R of the Long Mynd and, if the season is right, gathering what hazel nuts the squirrels might have left on your path.

5. Through the gate, keep straight on until you pass over the CG again near Comley Farm to return to your start.

If you are returning to Church Stretton via Walk A6, re-trace your steps to Point A on A7 sketch and then continue with the directions for Walk A6 from para. 9.

B. CRAVEN ARMS AREA

Craven Arms can scarcely be called 'hill country' but the operative word for this section is 'area'. Craven Arms itself is the nearest town to the small group of hills chosen here for walking and of all walks in this volume, perhaps these are the easiest. Some readers may be critical in that no walks to the east of the town are included; Wenlock Edge being conspicuous by its absence. The reason for this is space and, one has to admit, a certain preference. Perhaps another book can include that land but here, we have to contend ourselves with the lesser known delights of that pastoral area to the west of the town; that lying between Craven Arms and Bishop's Castle.

The area is dotted with villages and hamlets and intersected by small and delightful streams and rivers like River Clun and East Onny. The villages one passes through or by each have something worthy of note to offer whether it be a church, an unusual building or two or historical association — like Hopton Castle — or unusual traditions, like the annual tree-dressing at Aston-on-Clun.

The walking is easy, the scenery restful; nowhere should you feel isolated but everywhere you should feel the peace of, so far, an undiscovered area of rural England.

Walks B1, B2 and B3 can be done singly, in a pair or all together. If all are done, there is a total of about 10 miles — a good day — walk. Individually, each would be an enjoyable ramble with good views.

B1 Hopesay Hill-Hopesay-Hopesay Hill

Start & Finish: Lane from Craven Arms to Edgton.
Grid Ref.SO 403846.
Approx. Distance: 3 miles
Approx. Time: 1½ hours
Grade: Easy.
Pub/Café availability: Nearest — The Kangaroo at Aston-on-Clun. (Approx. 1½ miles South).
What to watch out for: Hopesay Church with its fine old lychgate with four gables, square tower begun in the 13th C. and topped with its wooden turret in the 17th C. 13th C. priest's doorway and chancel arch. The panels in the choir are Jacobean and there is glorious Medieval woodwork in the nave roof. The village of Aston-on-Clun sports two unusual round stone houses and Hopesay, a charming Rectory.

1. Enter Hopesay Common from the lane at the start by passing through wooden gate. Follow line of hedge on your L, climbing slightly until you reach the next wooden gate — a well made 5-bar — and enter Hopesay Common. (NT sign).

B1

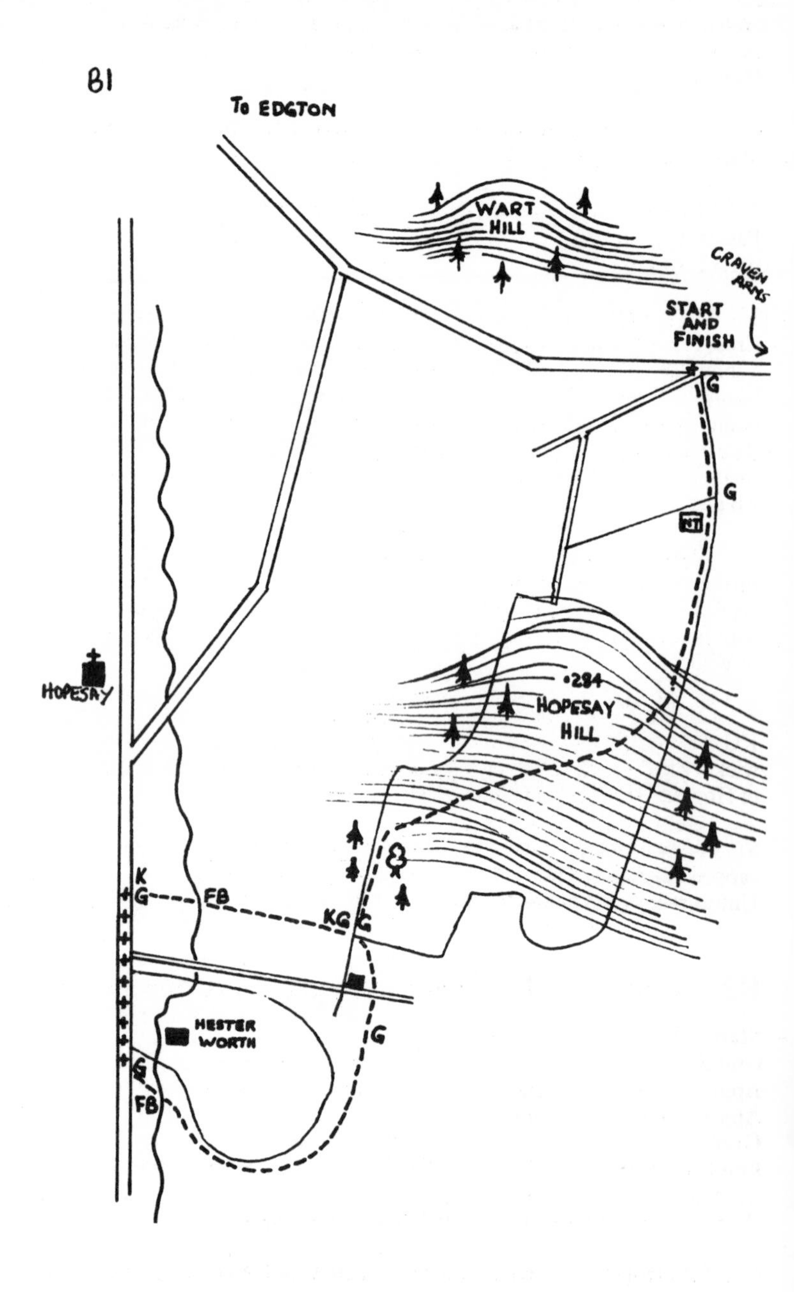

TO EDGTON
WART HILL
CRAVEN ARMS
START AND FINISH
G
G
NT
•284
HOPESAY HILL
HOPESAY
K
G
FB
KG
G
G
HESTER WORTH
G
FB

2. Keeping to line of fence, continue but very gradually bear R to crown of hill, following grassy track through bracken lines. Enjoy the extensive views about you and as you reach the top you will see Hopesay village tucked below you.

3. From top, bear slightly L down through bracken towards a clump of trees between you and the village.

4. You will reach a fence and you should spot a white wicket gate. Pass through this and follow line of path, now contouring the lower part of the hill.

5. The path takes you past a cottage on your R and you enter a track. Cross this and take gate opposite. Continue in same direction, climbing a shoulder of a field slightly. Soon you should see a large house and beautiful garden below you on your R. This is Hesterworth House, the home of Mr & Mrs V & J Richards. They let large and small holiday flats in the name of Hesterworth Holidays in this lovely valley. Skirt their garden boundary which will bear R eventually, taking you over a FB and you enter the lane via an iron KG.

6. Turn R along the lane past Hesterworth House and about 25 yards further on, take the iron KG into the field on your right. (Before leaving the lane, a short walk will take you into the village of Hopesay with its PO, lovely church and houses as well as, if you wish, the start of Walk B2).

7. Cross FB in field and bear R up hill to corner of field and another KG. Pass through this and immediately turn L through the white wicket gate of earlier. Re-trace your steps, puffing slightly, to the top of Hopesay Hill again and to the start.

8. As you come down to the end of the walk, you will see a wood-capped hill ahead. This is Wart Hill which sports an ancient fort. Unfortunately, no public footpath exists to its summit.

B2 Hopesay-Burrow-Kempton-Hopesay

Start & Finish: Hopesay Church.
Grid Ref.SO 390834
Approx. Distance: 5 miles
Approx. Time: 2½ hours
Grade: Moderate. Forestry tracks tend to be muddy.
Pub/café availability: Nearest — The Kangaroo Inn at Aston-on-Clun. (Approx. 1½ miles S of Hopesay).
What to watch out for: Hopesay Church. (See Walk B1).

1. With Hopesay Church on your L, take the track ascending slightly and at first fork, keep R on main track.

B2

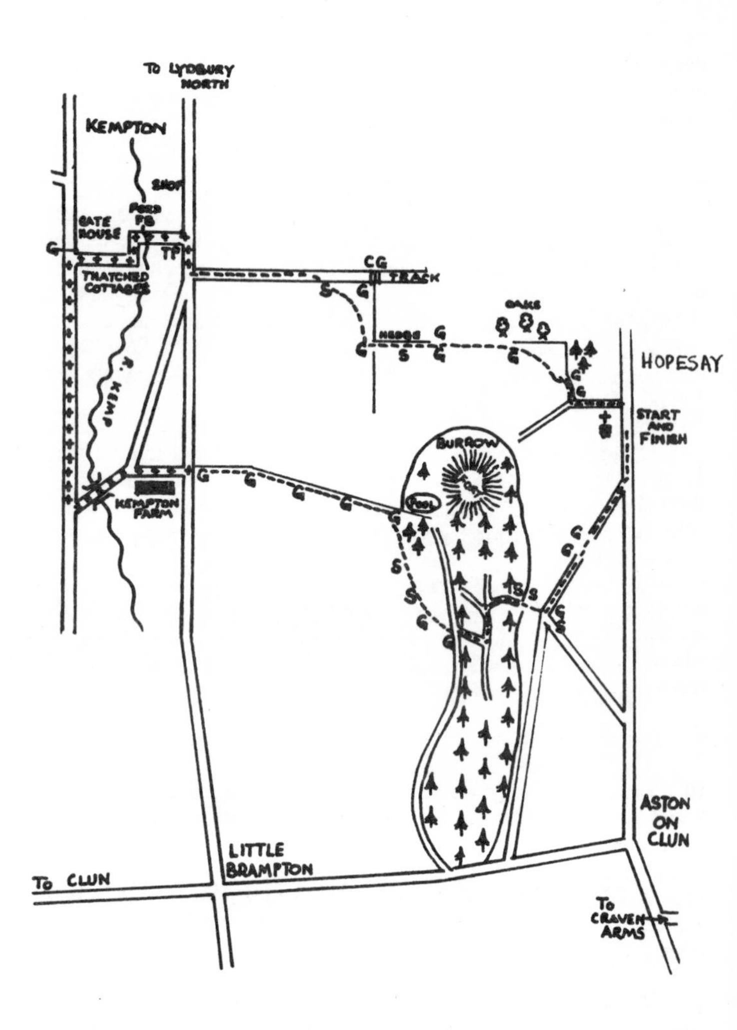
TO LYDBURY NORTH
KEMPTON
FORD
FB
GATE HOUSE
TF
THATCHED COTTAGES
CG
TRACK
HEDGE
OAKS
HOPESAY
START AND FINISH
BURROW
POOL
R. KEMP
KEMPTON FARM
LITTLE BRAMPTON
TO CLUN
ASTON ON CLUN
TO CRAVEN ARMS

2. Pass through two gates, skirt a small plantation on your R and ascend a meadow, bearing L, towards a stand of mature oaks in the corner by a gate.

3. Through G, bear L uphill across a field until you reach the opposite boundary and a pair of gates, side by side. Take L-hand gate and, keeping the hedge on your R, cross the next field to a S. As you walk, on your L will be the tree-covered slopes of the ancient Burrow Hill camp and, if you glance behind, Hopesay Hill will be seen.

4. Over the S, continue in the same direction to a G.

5. Pass through G and turn R. Stay in this field, keeping hedge on your R and when nearly at opposite boundary (you will see a G) bear L to a S in the hedge about 30 yards to the L of the G. Cross S and enter stony track.

6. Turn L and stay on this track — part of 'The Shropshire Way' — and enjoy the wide views as you gradually descend to the road at Kempton.

7. At road, turn R and then first L past the TP. This lane takes you through a ford — use FB — and, twisting, the lane passes a delightful collection of cottages, two of which are beautifully thatched.

8. If you are linking this walk with B3 at T junction turn R and almost immediately pass through a G in the lane next to Lodge House. If you are returning to Hopesay, turn L and follow lane to the next T junction where, turn L into a more major lane, passing over a bridge until you reach a fork by Kempton Farm.

9. Turn R at fork and in a few yards you reach the 'main' road.

10. Cross road and go through G opposite. Keep fence/hedge on your L and ascend gently towards Burrow Hill and wood passing through three more gates.

11. At end of fourth field from the road, you reach a gap near a small conifer plantation. Pass through gap and bear R uphill between the trees.

12. At top looking downhill, you should see the line of your descent which runs diagonally R through and over two stiles and two gates, the last gate being where you join the track through Burrow woodlands.

(If you miss your way at the top by the small conifers, you may have turned L and followed what seems to be an obvious track which brings you down to a pool and onto the same track. You will not be on a public right of way but if you turn R and keep along this track you will meet the G referred to above).

13. From gate, turn L up forestry track for only a few yards and then, turn R onto a grassy track through the trees which rises quite steeply.

14. At first junction, turn L. In a few yards, turn sharp R at a junction of three tracks. (The land-owners have marked the correct way 'footpath'). Follow this downhill through the trees to a stile. Cross S and enter sunken track at edge of wood.

15. At the next S, you enter a sunken 'green lane' which descends alongside a sheep-grazed meadow.

16. At field boundary you will see another S ahead. Do NOT take this, but turn L, through a G and enter another field on what resembles a bridle path.

17. Some care is necessary in route-finding but you should have no problems if you follow the same direction through the next few fields until you enter a 'proper' track which soon brings you to the lane at Hopesay. Turn L and return to start by the Church.

Hopesay Church (B2)

B3 Kempton-Clunton Hill-Merry Hill-Kempton

Start & Finish: Kempton Village.
Grid Ref. SO 361831
Approx. Distance: 2 Miles
Approx. Time: 1 hour
Grade: Easy
Pub/Café availability: See B2
What to watch out for: Abundant wild flowers (wood sorrel, foxgloves, meadowsweet, wood aven, etc.) in forest/woodland. Buzzards, kingfisher from bridge near Kempton Farm. Also, although the path does not take you there directly and it is not open to the public, there is Walcot Hall in whose grounds you walk. This was built for one of Shropshire's most famous sons — Robert Clive — Clive of India. The place-name Walcot (one of four in the county) is derived from 'walk', a derogatory term used by the Saxons for the Celts and indicates that Walcot was a Celtic settlement which survived the Saxon invasion and remained occupied by the native Britons for some time afterwards.

1. With TP at Kempton on your L take turning L and enter lane. Follow this, cross FB by a ford as the lane twists and turns past a cluster of cottages. Note in particular, the two good thatches as you approach the T junction.

2. At junction turn R almost immediately passing through a wooden gate by a lodge house. You now enter part of the Walcot Estate.

3. Go along the drive until you reach a fork and turn L.

4. Take first exit L through a gate and enter another track which ascends and curves gently towards woodland.

5. At entrance to woods, notice the beautiful mature chestnut near the track on your L and near the gate. Pass through gate and continue ascent on track as it curves R and a little further, L.

6. Immediately after curving L, you should see a path rising steeply on your L passing through the trees. Take this and keep on the path until your way is crossed by a wider, grassy track. The ascent to this is fairly steep and, particularly in high summer, tends to be obscured in part with undergrowth.

7. The public right of way continues straight ahead at the track, still ascending but the way becomes very overgrown. However, if you persevere and keep in straight line, you should reach the edge of this path of forestry where it is fenced. You should also find a stile in the fence. (If at the last track junction you have turned L, you should keep on this until your way is crossed by another more distinct track where you should turn R and in a few yards pass through a gate at A on sketch. Proceed along side of field, keeping fence on your L until you reach a stile in that fence).

B3

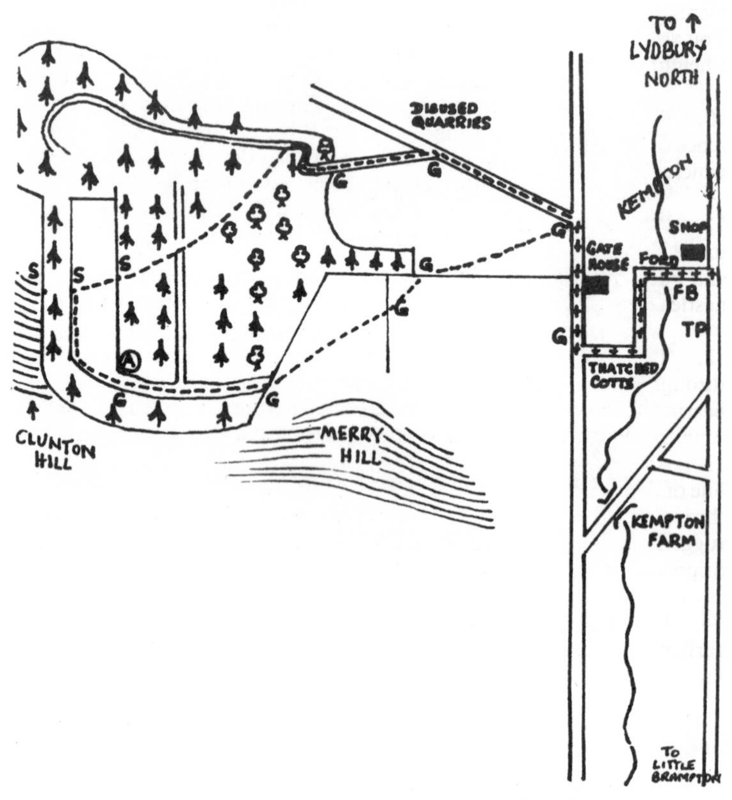
WALCOT
WALCOT PARK
TO ↑ LYDBURY NORTH
DISUSED QUARRIES
KEMPTON
SHOP
GATE HOUSE
FORD
FB
TP
THATCHED COTTS
CLUNTON HILL
MERRY HILL
KEMPTON FARM
TO LITTLE BRAMPTON
TO PURSLOW

8. If you have boldly gone where you may think no man (or woman) has gone before and found the stile at the top of the overgrown path in 7 above, you should cross this and head in the same direction across the field to the stile in the fence opposite (referred to in last line of 7 above).

9. Once you have recovered from the fever of route-finding here, you will realise that you have stopped climbing and seem to be on a plateau. You are. Climb over the last mentioned stile and enter a small section of woodland and, keeping in same line of direction, make for another stile in the opposite fence at the edge of the coppice. Here is a good picnic stop where you can enjoy fine views westwards and to the south. You are as near as a public footpath will take you to Clunton Hill and at a height of about 340 m. (1,115 ft.).

10. Re-trace your steps to stile on side of glade and turn R, keeping fence of wood on your R and head for gate A. You enter a good track which descends to the edge of this plantation where you meet a gate.

11. Pass through gate and enter field. Ahead now you should be able to see Titterstone in the far distance with heavily wooded Burrow Hill and Fort a little nearer. You are now on Merry Hill and before you nestles little Kempton.

12. This is a lovely section of the walk and well worth the battle through the footpaths of earlier. You descend by crossing the field bearing slightly L until you reach a gate in a fence.

13. After passing through gate, you continue in the same diagonal/left line of descent with the edge of the woods on your L and soon pass through an iron gate. By now you should have good views on your L of rugged Caradoc, the Long Mynd (very long from this angle), toothy Stiperstones and bold Corndon.

14. Continuing your descent, reach a gate on the track/drive of earlier. Turn R and re-trace your steps. If you have the time, linger by the tiny river and try to spot a kingfisher.

C. The Clee Hills

These hills comprise Titterstone Clee, Clee Burf and Abdon Burf. The two Burfs together known as Brown Clee, Abdon being the highest hill in Shropshire, indeed, in the Midlands of England. Geologically, The Clees are sandstone capped with a layer of harder basalt known as 'dhustone' (a derivation from the Cymraeg 'ddu' meaning in English 'black') and an excellent road stone. The basalt also accounts for the distinctive craggy appearance of the hills, particularly, Titterstone and although, in geological terms, 'young', they were certainly formed before the Ice Age. When the ice retreated, man could move north and therefore there are no signs of any prehistoric settlements before early Ice Age.

Since 1235 these hills have given a wealth of minerals — coal, limestones, iron, basalt and copper — and consequently have been much used and abused by man. Nowadays, the only active quarrying takes place on Titterstone and that is limited to roadstone. Mercifully, there is no longer any industrial quarrying on Brown Clee.

Although Abdon Burf lays claim to the highest summit at 1,790 ft. from most angles Titterstone's 'high- reared' dome seems higher and is more distinctive in shape. Titterstone's name is allegedly derived from a large rocking stone which stood amidst slabs of rock — 'totterstone'. The fort atop Titterstone is one of the largest and highest hill-forts in England and unusual because it has no ditch ramparts like so many of its age; some traces of the original protective walls have been found. The site covers almost eighty acres and dates from the Iron Age and possibly earlier. Sadly, most traces of fortification have been destroyed by quarrying and more lately be-decked with Civil Aviation radar domes and aerials. The ancient and modern stamp of man is indelibly, and not very prettily, imprinted on poor Titterstone.

Also, the Iron Age forts on Brown Clee are not so easily identified but the fort on lower Nordy Bank on the slopes of Clee Burf is more readily distinguishable and well-preserved.

The Clee's environs include numerous sites of deserted medieval settlements; villages which, like many in the Marches, shrank during the Middle Ages due mainly to the Black Death and later to agricultural decline following a succession of bad harvests. The following walks contain reference and include one or two of these vanished settlements.

The hills themselves had their own distinctive settlements through the ages and at one stage during the 1890's it was estimated that the Clee Hill industries employed about 2,000 people out of which sprang — and to an extent, still remains — a community with its own dialect and customs.

Work, prosperity, famine, plague and gradual decline have not treated the Clees lightly. Even war left its ugly mark as evidenced by the memorial tablet on Brown Clee to the memory of 23 German airmen who died in flying accidents on the hills between 1939 and 1945. Titterstone has the largest surviving community at Clee Hill village itself comprising many 'old' Clee families whose numbers are being boosted by the immigration of retiring Black Country and Birmingham folk while many of the villages around Brown Clee are being occupied by holiday-cottage owners.

The Clees may lack the pastoral solitude of some of the more remote South Shropshire hills, but they more than make up for this with their height, impressive shape and their character and 'feel' induced by years of human activity. Above and through it all, they have remained dignified and defiantly superior among Shropshire's hills: long may they remain so.

C1 Titterstone Circular

Start & Finish: Horseditch, Dhustone Quarry.
Grid Ref. SO 596773
Approx. Length: 6 miles
Approx. Time: 3 hours
Grade: Easy — unless you choose to scramble to the summit.
Pub/Café availability: The Victoria, The Royal Oak and The Angel pubs at Clee Hill village. Also, fish and chips at Clee Hill village — half mile north of Dhustone on main Ludlow/Kidderminster road.
What to watch out for: Site of Medieval deserted village at Cleestanton. Industrial history and archaeology such as disused Titterstone Incline rail track and old quarry workings.
N.B. *This walk is best attempted in clear conditions and in Spring or Autumn when the bracken is either so young as not to cause a problem or so old that its colour enhances your day. Towards the end of the walk, if you do decide to scramble to the trig point on the summit please take great care and do not go alone or in misty conditions because, even though you are not far from 'civilisation' the hill is treacherous in bad weather.*

1. By car, leave the main Ludlow/Kidderminster road west of Clee Hill village by turning up a lane sign-posted 'Dhustone'. Park below summit and entrance to old Dhustone Quarry; there should be sufficient room on a small lay-by which bridges a small stream. From here, head NE (keeping a line of telegraph poles on your L) across a pathless section of tussocky grass and moorland, keeping the summit of the hill on your L, until you reach a corner of a fence.

2. Turn L along a narrow track as it skirts the lower slopes of the hill. Gradually Brown Clee will come into view ahead and the spire of Cleeton St. Mary's Church below you on your R — and always the high, brooding profile of Titterstone on your L; radar domed and aerieled.

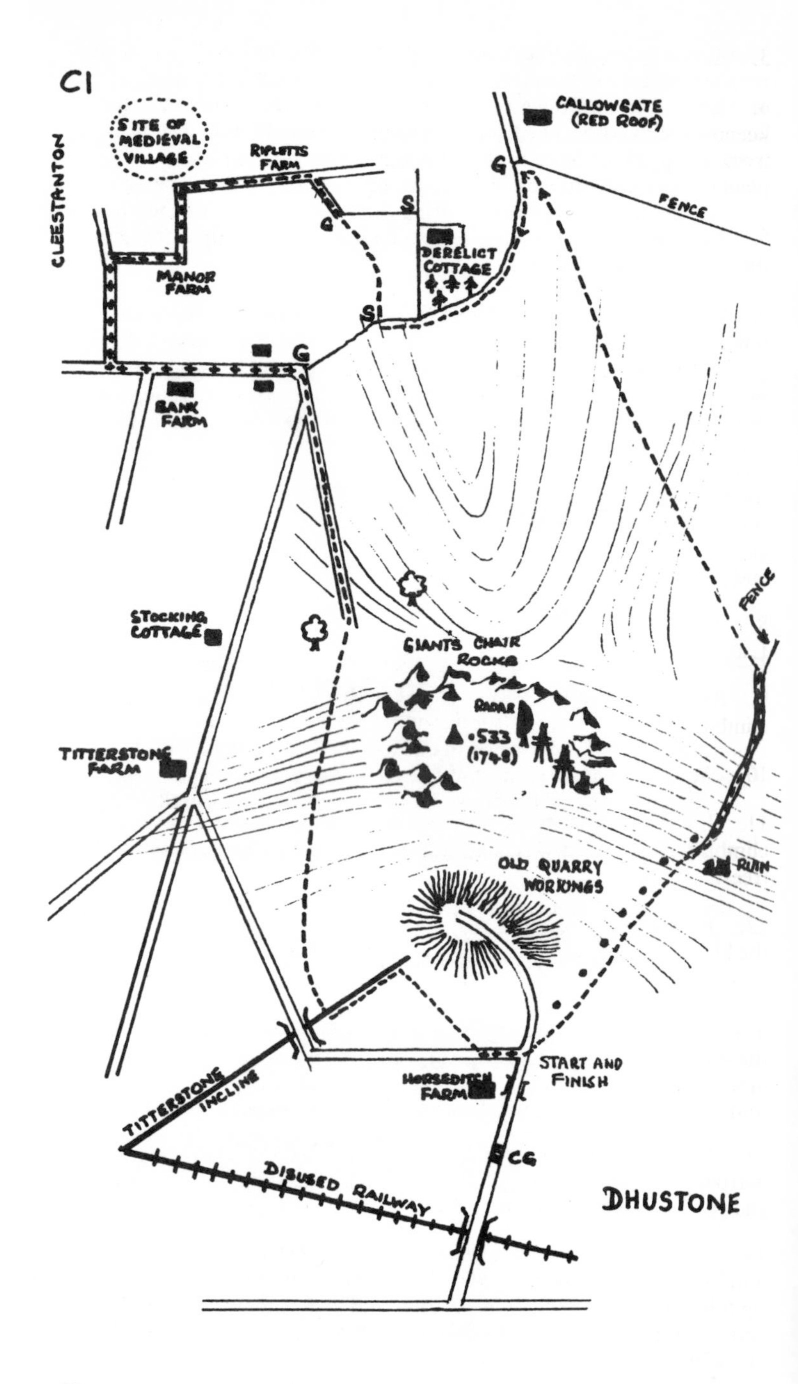
C1
SITE OF MEDIEVAL VILLAGE
CLEESTANTON
RIPLETTS FARM
CALLOWGATE (RED ROOF)
G
FENCE
S
G
DERELICT COTTAGE
MANOR FARM
S
G
BANK FARM
STOCKING COTTAGE
GIANTS CHAIR ROCKS
RADAR
·533 (1748)
TITTERSTONE FARM
FENCE
RUIN
OLD QUARRY WORKINGS
START AND FINISH
HORSEDITCH FARM
TITTERSTONE INCLINE
CG
DISUSED RAILWAY
DHUSTONE

3. As you skirt the hill make for the red roof of a cottage ahead.

4. Just before you reach the cottage, turn L at a fence and follow this, keeping it on your R, as you head towards a derelict cottage in some trees. Keep to the boundary fence as you skirt a small conifer plantation. (High Titterstone still on your L).

5. At the end of the plantation cross the stile in the fence and descend the field, crossing diagonally L to the opposite corner.

6. Cross gate and enter a stony track in a sunken lane. Follow for a few yards until it joins a better track.

7. Turn L onto this track and continue past two farms as the road improves in quality and ends in a T junction at the village of Cleestanton. (Note: At the sharp LH bend in the lane just before the second farm — Manor Farm — the fields on your right are the site of the Medieval deserted earlier village but this is barely discernable on site. Also, at Manor Farm, the north-western face of Titterstone is high above you, your view for once not marred by radar domes or quarries and you can appreciate what an impressive hill this is).

8. At the T junction in the village, turn L and at next T junction turn L again.

9. At next junction carry straight on up a longish, straight lane as you climb passing Bank Farm on your R.

10. At a gate, turn R along a grassy track which swings to the right.

11. In a few yards, take the grassy path L up through the bracken climbing all the way and passing between two fairly large hawthorn trees.

12. Eventually, your way levels out as you contour the lower slopes of the hill. Here you can enjoy the magnificent views West over Ludlow, Bringewood, High Vinnalls and on to the massed mountains of Wales beyond. This is a truly glorious end to a sunny day as the western lands lie ethereal in the fading light. You can deviate here by scrambling to the summit over the upturned, large rocks. If you do, then you can descend from the summit into the old Dhustone Quarry where you will find a tarmac lane which will take you back to your start.

13. If you keep on the lower slopes, you will find that the path narrows considerably through the bracken but keeps to the same height and you pass above a cottage and a farm below on your R.

14. You reach the grassy, disused railway workings known as Titterstone Incline which used to serve the quarry. Turn L along and up this for a while — about 50 yards — and then leave by turning R and follow the earlier contouring line direct to reach the tarmac road and your start.

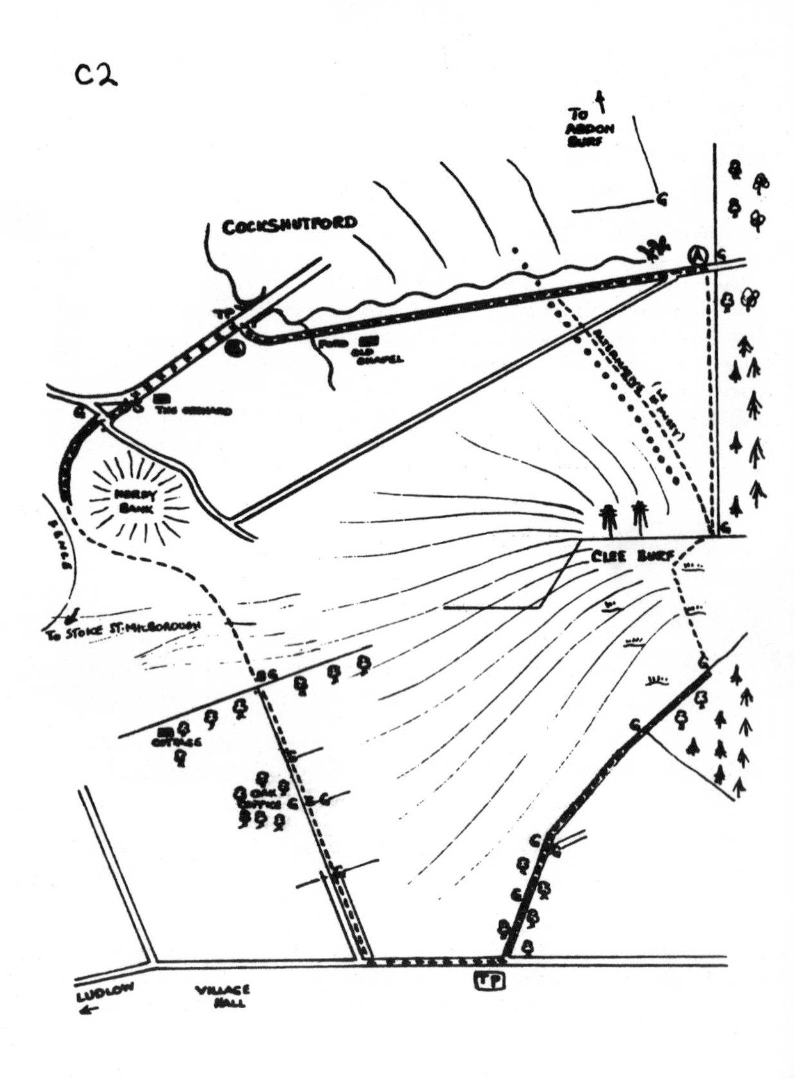
C2
To ABDON BURF
COCKSHUTFORD
TP
FORD
OLD CHAPEL
CLEE BURF
FENCE
To STOKE ST. MILBOROUGH
COTTAGE
LUDLOW
VILLAGE HALL
TP

C2 Clee Burf-Nordy Bank

Start & Finish: Thorn Lane, East of Stoke St. Milborough.
Grid Ref. SO 591828
Approx. Distance: 5 miles
Approx. Time: 2½ hours
Grade: Moderate. Good tracks but brackeny in parts in high summer.
Pub/Café availability: None within easy reach
What to watch out for: Clee Burf fortifications dating from pre-historic times and whose earth ramparts are still distinguishable despite quarrying. Nordy Bank fortifications which also date from pre-historic times but which are far better preserved having been untouched by industry; note single bank and ditch. Stoke St. Milborough — the nearest village although not on the route of the walk below unless you deviate. Known as 'Godestock' in the Domesday Book. Brook near church is named St. Milburga's Well after a grand- daughter of Saxon King Penda who escaped from a perilous pursuit here. Her horse's hoof sharply struck a stone from which a spring then rose. The church was dedicated to her and her horse. Note its 600 year old tower and fine Norman chancel.
N.B. *This walk can be linked with C3 at A on sketch and rejoining at B to make a total of about 9 miles and taking in the whole of Brown Clee, i.e. Clee Burf and Abdon Burf.*

1. There is limited parking at the start next to telephone box. (Take care not to block farmer's access to nearby field). Take sunken lane opposite TP box rising steadily. You are on part of the 'Shropshire Way' as evidenced by the buzzard way-mark signs you should see on your way.

2. Keep on uphill through two gates. (At second gate, take that on your L — there are a pair of gates here). Gradually, the path opens up slightly and looking backwards, Titterstone's noble profile can be seen, lying like an animal surveying its domain.

3. At the third gate, you meet a plantation on your R. Keep this to your R and where you reach a gate in the fence on your R, strike L (NW) diagonally following a narrow path through heather, marsh and whinberries towards the twin navigational masts atop your objective.

4. Do NOT deviate and eventually you find yourself climbing over the grass-covered rampart and ditch of the ancient Clee Burf fortifications and settlement. You are now at your highest point on this walk 510 m. or 1,673 ft.

5. With the masts on your L, pass through gate in fence. Far ahead, rises Abdon Burf and below to your L the patchwork of Wenlock Edge and the Stretton Hills beyond. (In very misty conditions, you can bear L around the masts and follow the line of some telegraph poles downhill through the bracken. The going is pathless but after the 14th pole you should meet a green track crossing your way. Here, turn L and follow on from directions at 7 below).

6. Through gate at 5 above, head along the top towards Abdon Burf by keeping a line of trees to your R and following these downhill slightly until you reach a gate in the fence on your R. Here you leave the 'Shropshire Way' (or go on with C3 walk if you wish) and you turn L and follow the lower grassy track downhill through the valley which you enter. (The higher track will take you straight to Nordy Bank but you will miss Cockshutford).

7. Near the valley floor, the grassy track joins a stream on your R and you run parallel with this for about a mile until you reach the lane at Cockshutford, passing on your way a sad little ruin of a Primitive Methodist Chapel and fording a tiny stream.

8. At lane, turn L and after half a mile take stile on your L after passing a house called 'The Orchard' on your L. Pause on the stile and look straight ahead to the view of the Black Mountains in a lovely mauve line on the horizon.

9. Over the stile, keep in same direction, crossing a track and skirt Nordy Bank which rises on your L. Contour this, keeping it on your L and all the time bearing L and following a grassy track. The path stays quite low and soon a fence joins you on your R. Keep straight on when fence turns R walking uphill on a path through the bracken. (If you

Clun Bridge (D5)

want to leave paths and tracks and visit Stoke St. Milborough, follow the fence R down a valley until you eventually reach a lane where, turn L and pass through the village. At T junction after the village turn L and pass the new village hall on your R and eventually reach the start).

10. At the top of the incline in the bracken path you should see the tips of the masts coming into view again and to your R, some trees on the skyline. The path is narrow and quite indistinct in places here through heather now. When the line of trees becomes clearer, bear R. When you reach a broader grassy track which crosses your way, turn R along this and you will reach the trees at a fence where you should also find a gate and a stile, side by side. You are back on the 'Shropshire Way'.

11. Take the stile and, keeping the fence you now find on your R, keep in this line of direction passing on your way over more stiles (2) and one gate before the final descent down a sunken 'green' lane to the lane of your start. (This section is perhaps the loveliest part of this walk being easy underfoot and giving marvellous views West and South).

12. At the lane, turn L and in quarter of a mile you reach your start.

C3 Cockshutford-Abdon Burf-Abdon-Cockshutford

Start & Finish: Cockshutford.
Grid Ref. SO 580851
Approx. Distance: 4½ miles
Approx. Time: 2½ hours
Pub/Café availability: None
Grade: Easy/moderate
What to watch out for: Wild Thyme, dragonflies, kestrels, buzzards, larks, pippits. In July and August — whinberries near summit. Medieval village at Abdon — there are distinct house platforms visible. The village's decline was gradual during the Middle Ages. It was re-occupied to house employees of Brown Clee mines and quarries in 16th and 17th C. but deserted again in late 18th C. with the decline of these industries. Pre-historic settlement of Abdon Burf.
N.B. *This walk takes you to the top of the highest hill in the county with a height of 1,772 ft. The views are extensive and cover most of the western part of central England, the Welsh Berwyns, Brieddens, Wenlock Edge, the Stretton hills, the Long Mynd, the faint outlines of distant Cadair Idris and the Plinlimon round to the Black mountains and Brecon Beacons in South Wales.*

1. Park opposite TP kiosk in Cockshutford in a small layby. With the brook on your left, take 'green lane', climbing gradually at first. Here, in summer, wild thyme grows in abundance on the banks on your L. You also pass on your way the ruin of a tiny Primitive Methodist chapel on your R.

C3

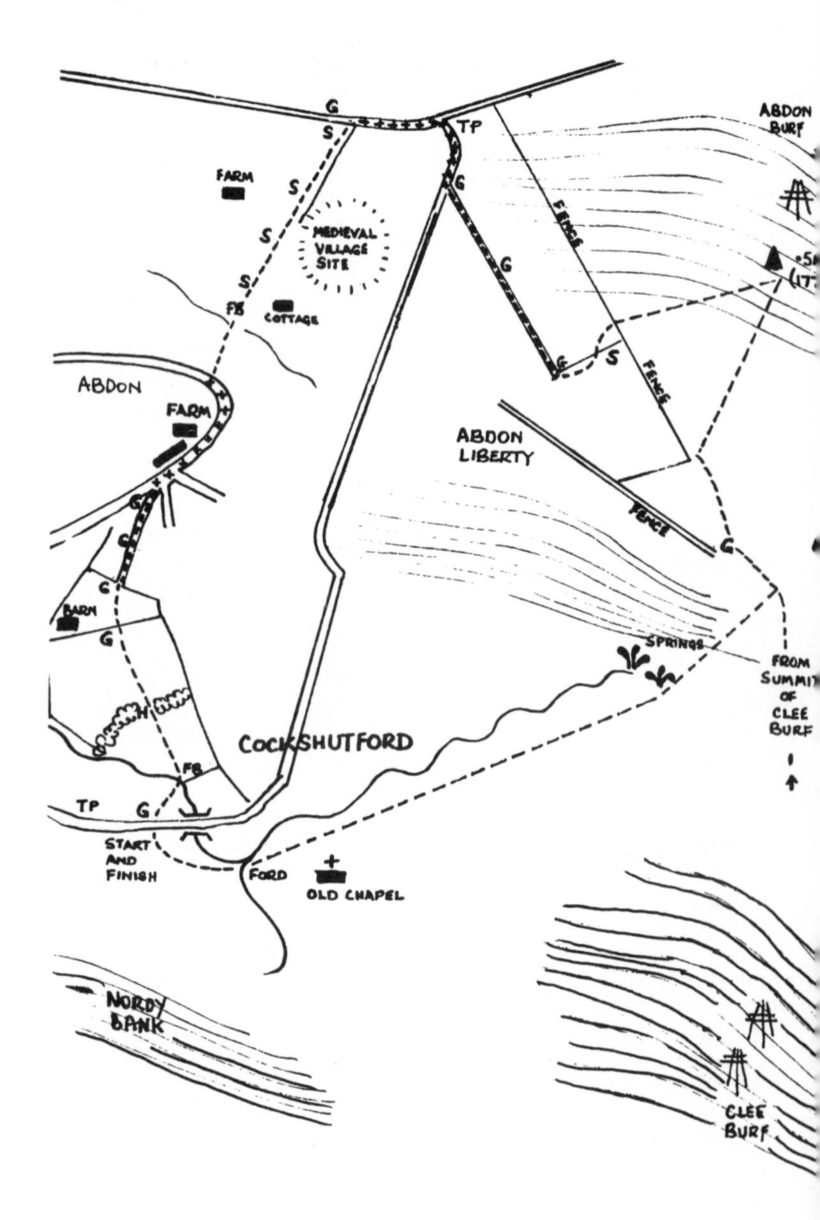
ABDON BURF
TP
G
S
FARM
MEDIEVAL VILLAGE SITE
FENCE
FB
COTTAGE
ABDON
FARM
ABDON LIBERTY
BARN
SPRINGS
FROM SUMMIT OF CLEE BURF
COCKSHUTFORD
TP
START AND FINISH
FORD
OLD CHAPEL
NORDY BANK
CLEE BURF

2. Keep on this grassy track which soon begins to cut its way through bracken, the stream still on your L, and gradually you ascend to the head of the valley.

3. At the top, keep straight on towards the line of trees on the sky-line and when nearly there, turn L along a path to a gate which bears the Shropshire Way buzzard way-mark. Ahead now is twin-masted Abdon Burf.

4. Pass through the gate and take the path to your R, NOT that following the fence on your L. Your path ascends through heather and whinberries and soon you see the trig. point, masts and earthworks of the summit conglomeration as they come into view on your R. Below you on your L, Nordy Bank's well preserved ditches show distinctly.

5. You will now join a fence on your L. Here you can leave your main track and head NNE across the heather to your objective.

6. Leave the summit trig. point and return to the fence you left, bearing SW. You should reach the fence at a gap. (If in doubt, or misty, retrace your steps to the corner of the fence which you left earlier then turn R and follow the line of the fence on your L until you reach the gap).

7. Now, facing downhill, you will see a stile nearby on your L which bears a Shropshire Way way-mark. Strictly, you should cross this, turn R downhill with a fence on your R and in a few yards turn R through a gate and join a track. However, the most obvious way from the gap in the fence is straight downhill with fence which descends with you on your L. This is not the public right of way but is obviously well-used. Using this way, when you reach the gate which is on your L, turn R down the track. This is sunken and the banks on either side covered in wild thyme; a truly lovely descent of the hill. Follow this track until you reach the lane.

8. At lane, turn R and in a few yards, turn L after passing a TP kiosk on your R. In about 20 yards cross stile on your L in a hedge and, in field, follow this line of direction, keeping field fences on your L passing over three stiles, the latter part of this section being in a sunken green lane. Eventually, you cross a FB by a cottage, enter a lane which serves the cottage and soon you reach the road in the village opposite a farm. (On your L after the second stile on this section, the fields hide the remains of the Medieval village of Abdon).

9. At lane, turn L and opposite the last set of farm buildings (in about 50 yards) turn L. A choice of three gates confront you! Take the one on the R and the track for a while follows almost a parallel line with the lane which you have just left but gradually it veers away.

10. Pass through two gates and on entering a field, you will see some substantial stone barns. Take gate to the L of the LH barn and cross next field diagonally L to an iron hurdle set in the middle of a tall hedge.

11. Cross hurdle and make for RH corner of next small field. You should come to an old FB across a stream. (Take care if surface is wet!) Cross FB and turn L on a track to pass through a gate and to reach the lane opposite your start.

D. CLUN AREA

This area covers the large upland expanse of South West Shropshire from Bishop's Castle in the North to Bucknell in the South and bounded by Offa's Dyke westwards to Craven Arms in the east. Its two main towns — really more like large villages — are Bishop's Castle and Clun and lovely though they are, it is the countryside that reigns supreme. Most of the land is over 1,500 ft. high and is the most remote and perhaps the most beautiful in the county. Although individual hills may lack the height of, say, Brown Clee or the heathered expanses of the Long Mynd or the cragginess of Caradoc, they roll languidly along England's western reaches, timelessly tumbling in and out of their wilder neighbour, Cymru.

This part is known also as 'Clun Forest' although now, apart from the tracts of modern conifer and larch around Bucknell, there is much open hilly land. In the 16th C. the forest extended to some 17,000 acres and the red deer were well-hunted but the ancient meaning of 'forest' does not coincide with our present day visualisation of tree- ranked hills and moorland. Then, whilst it did include large sections of woodland, its principal meaning was a reserve or Royal hunting-ground.

Nowadays, the most evident animals are sheep. Lots of them! On your walks you will rarely be away from them. Indeed, when you leave the area and walk in other parts you may even miss their calm presence. You will see several different breeds including the white-faced and rather superior looking Border Leicesters; the pretty Beulah Speckled with their black eyes and noses and speckled faces and, of course, the area's own Clun breed distinctive with their black faces under a tuft of white fleece between black ears, white body and black legs. They are known throughout the world and, as well as being hardy and adaptable to different climates, they yield high-quality fleeces with wool that has good elasticity. It is thought that the original Clun sheep were bred by pastoral or semi-nomadic shepherds who lived in the Clun Forest about 1,000 years ago.

As you walk, beneath your feet and under the sheep-cropped grass or forestry track lies the heart of the land; mostly Silurian rock around the Bishop's Castle area and the next succeeding strata near Clun itself, namely Old Red Sandstone. Both very different in character, the latter contains traces of lime, a legacy of the sandy deposits from the Silurian

Clun Castle Ruins (D5)

sea, the huge lake which covered much of Wales and its Border Counties. The former was laid down about 400 million years ago; the latter, about 345-395 million years ago. Many feet must have trodden these hills since then but there are days with only sheep for company one could be forgiven for thinking that one is the first.

What a land! There are the hills which are be- darkened by the modern foresters' Sitka with much of the former wildlife gone but which yield sudden clearings and glorious views. There are the tranquil hamlets and, at present, 'un-twee' villages like jewels in the thread of the River Clun. Then, there are the upland lanes that wind and roll around and along the Dyke. To linger along the high, unhedged lanes around Newcastle-on-Clun is to experience a sense of exhilaration and intoxication that comes more often to hill-walkers in the remoter parts of Cymru, the North West of England or Scotland. Unlike those harsher hills, these are hospitable with their occasional homesteads and well-farmed high acres. One has the sense that the area has been mutedly, almost apologetically, farmed in exactly the same way since time began; a cared-for land used yet not abused; a high, wide land filled with western light and often, western moisture; patch-worked with a more caring hand of Man than evident on the Clees; a kind, lilting land that, in one's more sentimental moods, one would readily believe to be populated by kind people with lilting voices. The realist would argue that people are the same the world over. Perhaps the cynical view is correct but on Edenhope Hill on an April day it is very, very easy to believe otherwise.

D1

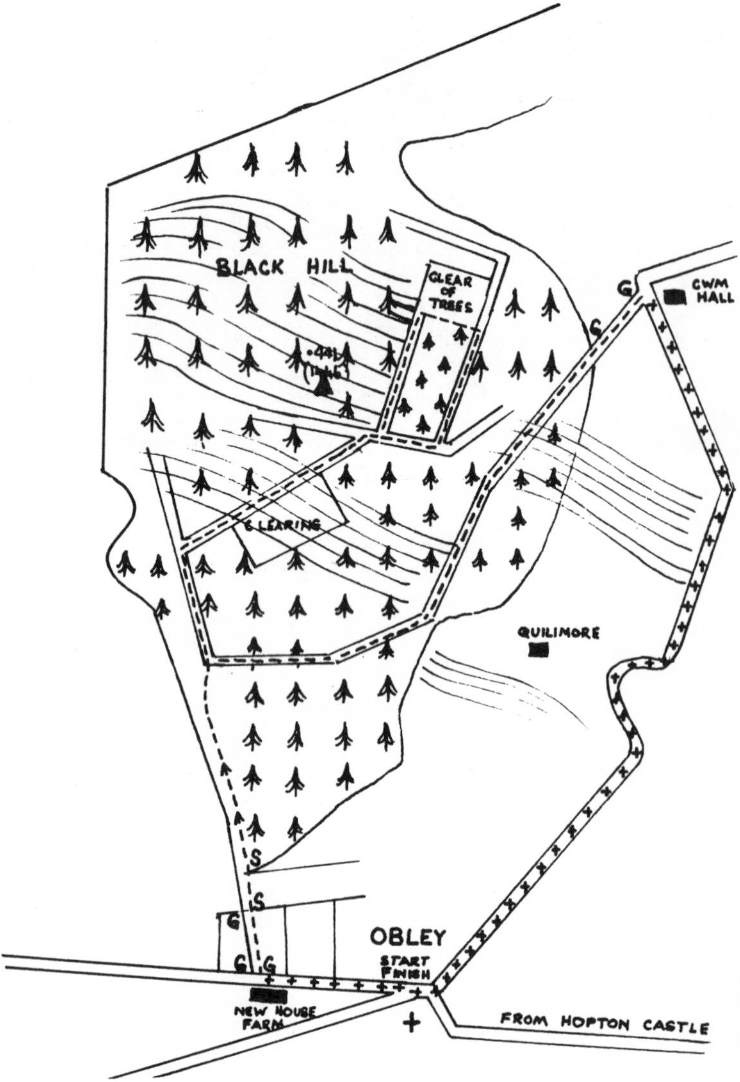

BLACK HILL

CLEAR OF TREES

CWM HALL

CLEARING

QUILIMORE

OBLEY

START FINISH

NEW HOUSE FARM

FROM HOPTON CASTLE

D1 Obley-Black Hill-Obley

Start & Finish: Obley.
Grid Ref. SO 332781
Approx. Distance: 2½ miles
Approx. Time: 1¼ hours
Grade: Easy apart from an initial steep, but short, ascent. A good walk for a fairly quickly gained viewpoint and picnic spot.
Pub/Café availability: Nearest at Clun — 2½ miles NW. The Sun Inn. Tea rooms between bridge and church.
What to watch out for: Whinberries in high summer. Buzzards & jays. Silurian rock outcrops in forest.

1. With the primitive Methodist Chapel (now a house) on your L, take fork in lane R and after 50 yards, take a gate on your R — opposite New House Farm.

2. In field, keep fence on your L and climb the meadows, crossing two stiles on your way.

3. Over the second stile, keep fence on your L, but climb more steeply on the edge of the forestry. (In July and August your way may be sweetened by whinberries).

4. At top, the path joins a forestry track. Turn L along the track. By now, the ascent will have eased and if you look to your L, you should see masted Black Mixen Hill near New Radnor, with Bache Hill to its L.

5. Take first turning R onto another forestry track and you soon pass by a clearing of trees on your R.

6. At end of the clearing and at the junction with another track, turn R and then, almost immediately, turn L and leave the well-made track you have been following and enter a grassy 'ride'. You are now very near the highest point of Black Hill, the trig. point being only a few yards away on your L in the thick firs. It is pointless to seek it out — the views are better later on. However, your height is about 1,440 ft.

7. The grassy ride peters out at another clearing and it is here that you can enjoy the views.

8. Turn R along the line of trees and as you walk the grassy, high single path, your gaze will be drawn to the wide vista on your L; from Corndon to Stiperstones, the Long Mynd and distinctive Caradoc and round to Brown Clee and Titterstone. On a good day, this is an ideal stop for a picnic.

9. The grassy path joins another forestry track. Turn R along this and keep on along it until you rejoin the spot where you left this track earlier. Then, back along this track, with the earlier clearing now on your L.

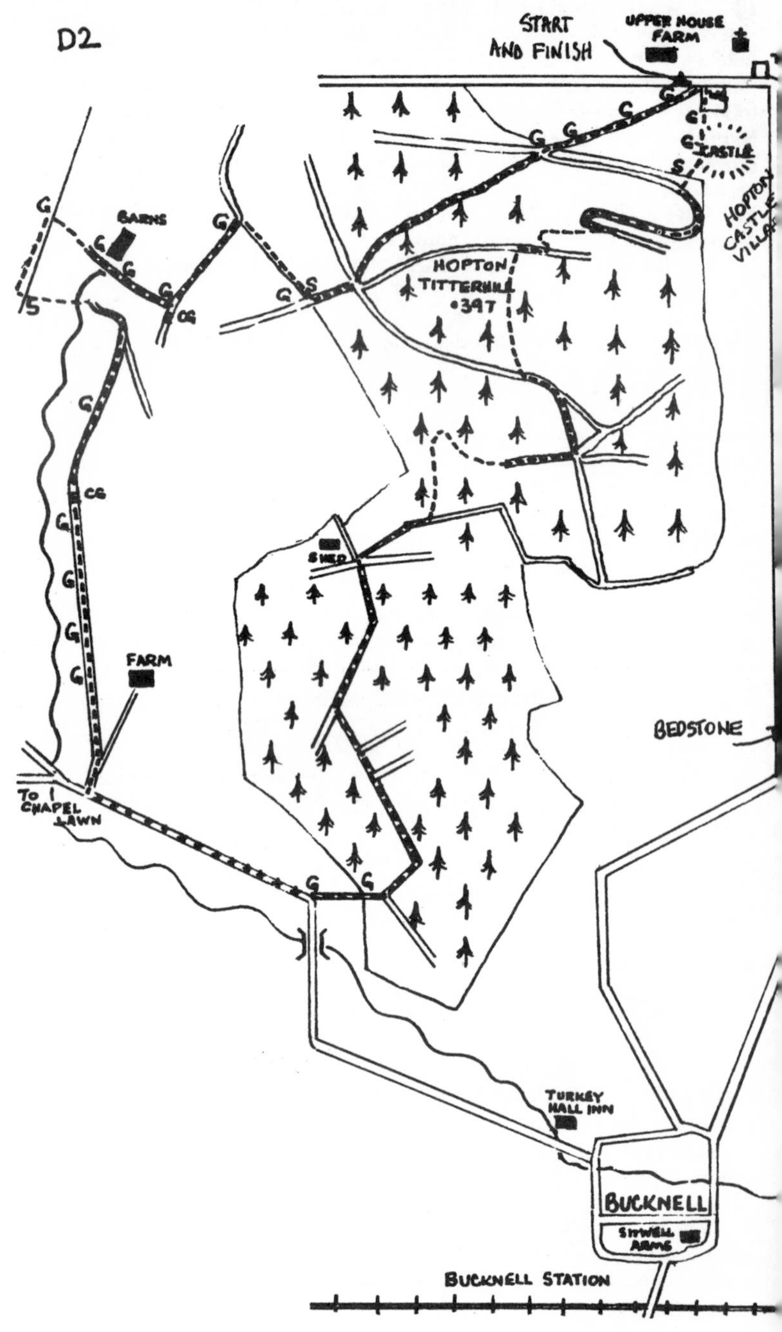
D2
START AND FINISH
UPPER HOUSE FARM
CASTLE
HOPTON CASTLE VILLAGE
BARNS
HOPTON TITTERHILL
•397
SHED
FARM
BEDSTONE
TO CHAPEL LAWN
TURKEY HALL INN
BUCKNELL
SITWELL ARMS
BUCKNELL STATION

10. After clearing, turn L at next T junction and after a few yards, you can either rejoin the steep path you took earlier and descend to the fields, over the two stiles and back to the lane and Chapel, or at the junction with the descending path, you can keep to the main track and follow this all the way to the lane at Cwm Hall. If you choose the latter, be prepared for quite a long walk through the forest but at least it is downhill all the way.

11. At the lane at Cwm Hall, turn R and keep on this lane until you reach your start.

D2 Hopton Castle-Bucknell Hill-Hopton Titterhill-Hopton Castle

Start & Finish: Hopton Castle village.
Grid Ref. SO 365782
Approx. Distance: 6 miles
Approx. Time: 3 hours
Grade: Moderate. Two long steep climbs — some overgrown paths, forestry walking and great care is necessary in following the directions in the forest.
Pub/Café availability: The Sitwell Arms and The Turkey Hall Inn at Bucknell 2½ miles South of Hopton Castle.
What to watch out for: Wild raspberries when in season; deer, hares, jays, buzzards, spotted and green woodpeckers. Hopton Castle — The remains of a Norman keep. Samuel More (whose family had held land in Shropshire since the Norman Conquest) was a strong Parliamentarian in the Civil War. In Feb. 1643 Cromwellians held out in Hopton Castle for a fortnight against the Royalists. The seige ended in the Parliamentarians surrender. More was taken to Ludlow Castle as a prisoner but 24 of his soldiers were horribly mutilated and buried alive here.

1. With TP kiosk in Hopton Castle village on your R, go up the lane and after passing Upper House Farm Guest House on your R, take track through the gate on your L.

2. Follow track passing through three more gates to enter forestry.

3. Stay on track and after the first RH bend, it starts to descend slightly. Before descending take grassy track through trees on your L. This rises and, in places, widens and is a long pull. Persevere until you reach a wider grassy track.

4. Turn R along this and at the junction of next, harder forestry track, keep straight on over this and pass through a gate. Stay on the track but you will notice that land on your R is now open. You are now at some 355 m. or 1,165 ft.

5. Before next gate (which leads to a farm) you should cross a stile in a fence on your R. You now enter a field and you should keep the fence now on your L until you reach another track. As you walk this stretch, you should have good views to your R of Stiperstones, the Long Mynd, Corndon and Stretton's Caradoc.

6. At track take a gate on your L and follow the track until you reach a gate and a CG and a fork in the track.

7. Take R fork towards some modern barns and pass through two more gates (one on each side of barns).

8. Stay on track and pass through a gate to enter a field above the barns.

9. In field you will see ahead of you some miles distant Stowe Hill and the earthwork of Caer Caradoc. Turn L and keep the fence on your L until you reach a stile in that fence.

10. Cross stile and descend the field, bearing L in a valley until you cross a stream (no FB) and enter a track which leads down from the barns.

11. Turn R and follow track, descending with the stream on your R.

12. Pass through a gate and enter a field. Keep in line with some telegraph poles and descend the valley until you reach another gate (old and next to an equally ancient CG). Pass through this and stay on track; the stream still below you on your R.

13. Pass through another gate and when the way forks a little later on, go R.

14. Pass through two more gates (on either side of some buildings and a litter of machinery) and enter a lane.

15. Turn L and go along lane until you reach a RH bend after a 'Danger' sign. Here you will see a gate on your L. Pass through this and enter a track.

16. At next gate, you enter forestry again and soon, at a fork where the main track follows the valley towards Bucknell, you turn L sharply and climb steeply through the trees on a grassy path for some time.

17. Your path is joined by two or more tracks coming from your R and at next junction turn R.

18. After a few yards, your track joins a harder, newer track. Turn L down this and walk until all tracks converge by a FC sign 'Hopton'. (You should also notice a shed in a field on your L). At this confluence, you should take the forestry track that goes R but downhill and stay on

this for one third to half mile until it bends quite sharply R. On bend, you should leave track and keep straight on up a narrow, often overgrown path up a V-shaped cutting in the hillside/forestry.

19. This path is steep and sometimes difficult to negotiate, but not impossible. Eventually, it levels onto a grassy, wider way and the trees clear a little.

20. At the next definite junction, turn L uphill and in a few yards you join a well-made forestry track.

21. Follow this uphill but when it turns to the L, you should keep straight on up the hill and onto quite a faint grassy track which narrows to an almost indistinct path. Your way is helped somewhat by the fact that this section is cleared of trees. You are now on Hopton Titterhill and as you begin to descend again, you should be able to see Brown Clee on your R and ahead, Caradoc (the one at Stretton) and the Stiperstones. This section is quite tricky underfoot because it is so little trodden and you have to watch out for broken branches under the long grass and tussocks.

22. The path joins an old forestry track. You turn R and in only 75 or so yards, turn L into the trees onto a hidden path which descends and broadens through woodland. This turns R on itself soon and, still descending through Spruce and Fir, you find that the path improves and you eventually reach another forestry track.

23. Turn L and follow until you reach the first sharp bend L. Here you leave the track and keep straight on — fighting your way through some undergrowth for a few feet — until you reach a fence on the edge of a field at which, by a shed, you should find a stile.

24. Cross stile and, below you lies Hopton Castle village and to its right, the Castle itself is clearly visible.

25. Heading in the direction of the village (not the Castle), cross the field to the next gate. Take this and keep straight on across another field, jumping over an open ditch on your way, and make for a small orchard.

26. Take gate into orchard; cross and leave orchard by a small wicket gate. You enter the lane in the village opposite the Church and return to your start.

N.B. *At 15, you could keep to the lane until you reach Bucknell some 1¼ miles away. Here pub refreshment is available and the village itself is worth a visit. You then return to point at No. 15 to rejoin the walk. This diversion would add 2½ miles to the complete walk.*

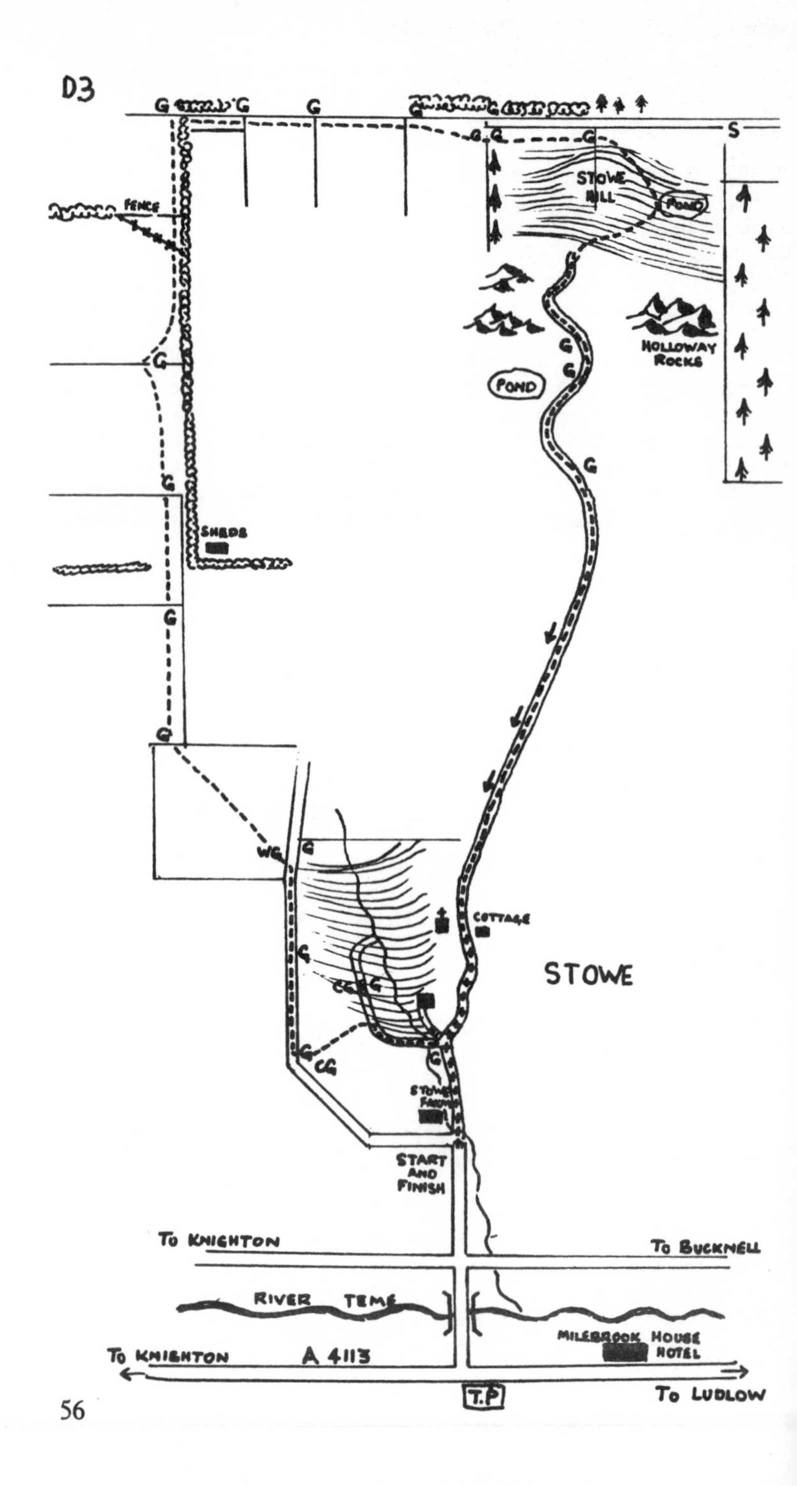
D3
G
G
G
G
G
G
S
FENCE
STOWE HILL
POND
G
G
HOLLOWAY ROCKS
POND
G
G
G
SHEDS
G
G
WG
G
COTTAGE
STOWE
G
CG
G
G
CG
G
STOWE FARM
START AND FINISH
To KNIGHTON
To BUCKNELL
RIVER TEME
MILEBROOK HOUSE HOTEL
To KNIGHTON
A 4113
T.P
To LUDLOW

he Long Mynd from above Norbury (E2)

D3 Stowe Hill

Start & Finish: Stowe Farm.
Grid Ref. SO 312736
Approx. Distance: 4 miles
Approx. Time: 2 hours
Grade: Moderate. A long climb near the start but good tracks and paths.
Pub/Café availability: Nearest pub — The Milebrook House on main Knighton road half mile from Stowe. Also cafes and pubs at Knighton — 1 mile W.
What to watch out for: First, you cannot help but admire Stowe itself; a delightful hamlet sheltered by the hill. Stowe Church — 13th C. inside; the roof's tie-beams, queen posts and decorative panelling. The roof is 17th C. The altar table is Jacobean. The setting is idyllic. Caer Caradoc — from Stowe Hill you will have a good view of this ancient hill-fort with very clear ramparts and ditches. Thought to be the spot where Caradoc (Caractacus) — the British leader who held out against the Romans in AD 50 — made his final stand. (The Caer Caradoc near Church Stretton and the Briedden Hills in Powys also lay claim to this).

1. Park below Stowe Farm and walk uphill along the lane. At first bend to the R, turn L, passing through a gate and enter a track which winds downwards towards a brook.

2. Cross brook and now leave track (before gate and CG) by turning sharp L and ascending and skirting a hillside in a meadow, bearing R as you do so.

3. At a gate and CG, you join a track which has ascended from the farm below. Pass through gate and climb quite steadily along a high, stony track. The views here open out on your L. Bache Hill and masted Black Mixen at New Radnor are clearly visible and below you, lies snug little Knighton town.

4. Pass through the next gate and continue uphill along the track enjoying the views to your L and the valley deepening below you on your R.

5. Immediately before the next gate, you will see a wicket gate in the fence on your L. (It may be decorated with barbed wire!). Climb this and enter a high field. Then, bear R diagonally across field to reach another gate in the opposite fence.

6. Pass through this gate and turn R, keeping fence (and later a hedge) on your R.

7. Keeping in the same direction, pass through another gate and eventually, you reach a barbed fence. Cross this and in only two or three yards, cross a fence into another field. Keep in same direction across this field and you soon reach a gate which you cross and enter a green track.

8. Turn R along the overgrown track and keep in this direction gently ascending Stowe Hill and passing through six more gates, all the time keeping the fence/hedge on your L. This is a lovely section and as you walk, your views to the N (your L) will include Stiperstones' jagged teeth on the skyline, the Long Mynd and the Stretton Hills including Caer Caradoc. Nearer to you and slightly below, you will also have good views of the other Caer Caradoc. (see note above).

9. After the sixth gate, still climbing (but gently) leave the fence line and bear slightly R across high meadow atop Stowe Hill and heading towards a plantation on the skyline. Shortly, you should reach an upland pond. This is an excellent picnic spot, weather permitting.

10. On leaving the pond, make for the highest point of the hill- top. (On a clear day, you will have excellent views of the mountains of South Wales). Then, head downhill towards Knighton town below you and join a sunken, ancient track that descends.

11. Follow this all the way back to Stowe, passing on your way beneath Holloway Rocks — a fine outcrop and quite unexpected on this so far rounded and pastoral hill. You pass through three gates and near the end of the track, you will see the beautifully situated Stowe Church on your R. If time permits, it is well worth a visit, if only to sit in its peaceful churchyard and soak in the tranquility.

12. The track joins a tarmac lane near the lychgate. Follow lane back and down to Stowe Farm.

D4 Mainstone-EdenhopeHill-Churchtown- Mainstone

Start & Finish: Mainstone village.
Grid Ref. SO 276877

Approx. Distance: 3 miles
Approx. Time: 1½ hours
Grade: Easy. Good paths and tracks.
Pub/Café availability: Several inns and at least two cafes at Bishop's Castle — 3 miles. The Sun Inn and Clun Bridge Cafe at Clun — 5 miles. The Crown Inn at Newcastle-on-Clun — 4 miles.
What to watch out for: Ravens. Mainstone Church (at Churchtown). This small village was once an important trading point. The name is derived from the Cymraeg 'Maen' meaning 'Stone'. On the floor by the pulpit in the Church is a boulder of granite worn smooth by the hands of a hundred years or more. Weighing 20 cwt. there is speculation that in trading times it was used as a weight but more lately acquired a reputation as a trial of strength for village youths who would hold it over their heads and toss it over their left shoulder. Of the Church, note the magnificent roof structure and, of course, idyllic position in a deep wooded valley across which runs the Offa's Dyke long distance footpath.

1. With the Primitive Methodist Church at Mainstone on your R, take track past this and begin to climb passing through a gate and follow the good track to some barns.

2. Passing the barns, continue up the track. Pass through a gate, turn R and follow fence until you see a gate on the L and on the opposite side of the field. Bear L diagonally across field to the gate. Pass through and enter a tarmac lane.

3. Turn L and walk this lane until it bends to the R. On your way you will pass and cross Offa's Dyke long distance Footpath. (You should see the 'acorn' waymark sign on two stiles; one on either side of your lane). This lane offers a high, panoramic walk with splendid open views in all directions. In particular, to your R you will distinguish Corndon, the Stiperstones ridge and behind you, the Long Mynd as you rise gently. To the far R on the horizon if conditions permit, you may be able to see the Welsh Berwyns and nearer to hand, the Brieddens. The road traverses Edenhope Hill and is the essence of this area of high, wide rolling hills. The highest point on the road is 406 m. (1,333 ft.) but the top of the hill itself at 424 m. (1,392 ft.) is in the fields on your L.

4. As the road bends to the R, you turn L through a gate and you enter a delightful grassy lane which keeps to approximately the same height. On a sunny day, this is a lovely place to stop to rest, have a snack or simply savour the views and solitude.

D4

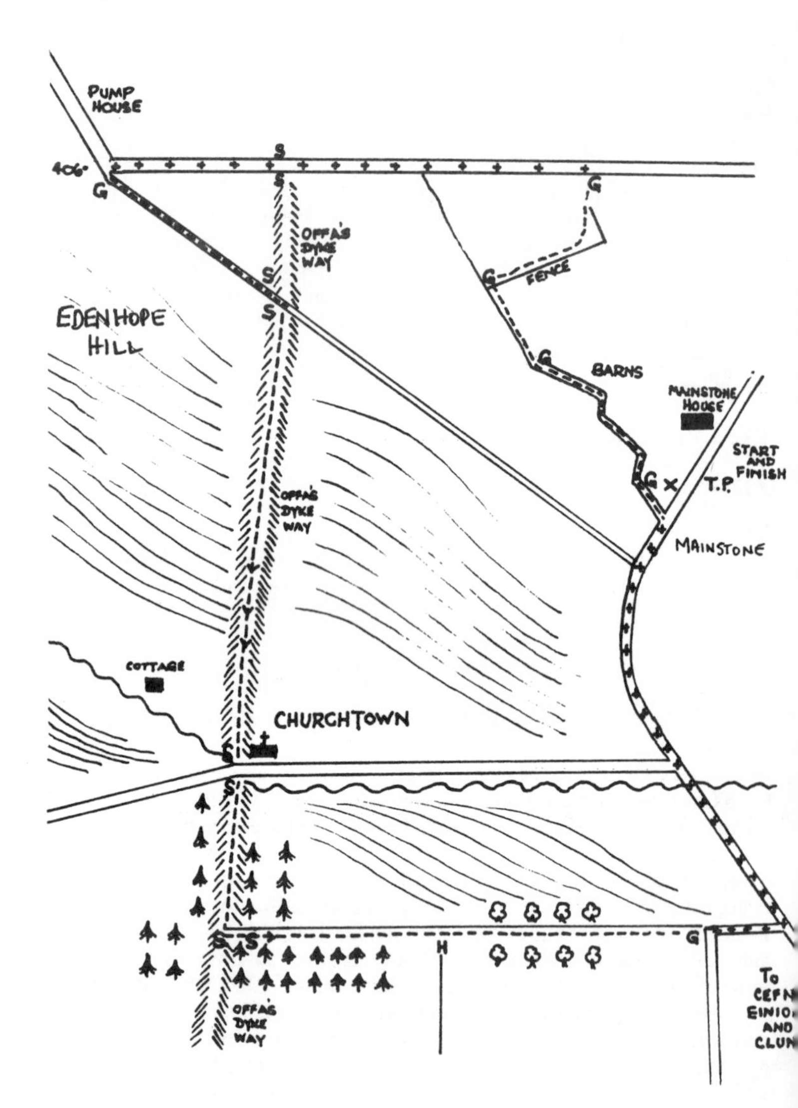
PUMP HOUSE
406°
G
S
S
G
OFFA'S DYKE WAY
G
FENCE
S
S
EDENHOPE HILL
G
BARNS
MAINSTONE HOUSE
START AND FINISH
G
T.P.
MAINSTONE
OFFA'S DYKE WAY
COTTAGE
CHURCHTOWN
S
S
S
S
H
G
OFFA'S DYKE WAY
To CEFN EINIO AND CLUN

5. As you begin to descend, keep a look-out for a stile on each side of the green lane, each bearing the 'acorn' waymark and take the stile on your R. Keep to the Offa's Dyke path and descend to join the lane in the valley at Churchtown. Divert, if you can, to look inside the church on your L.

6. Then take Offa's Dyke stile on other side of lane passing between barbed wire and a young fir tree plantation to another stile. Here, you leave the Offa's Dyke path and immediately turn L over another stile to enter a more well established plantation (you are now on part of the Shropshire Way).

7. Keep fence and edge of woodland on your L and follow grassy path — at times quite overgrown — along the line of the valley parallel to the lane to Mainstone and the small river below. You cross one hurdle-type fence on your way and after leaving the woods and contouring the hillside by way of overgrown meadows, you enter a lane.

8. Turn L and descend the lane to a T junction. Turn L and soon you reach your start.

D5 Whitcott Keysett-Weston Hill- Graig Hill-The Cefns (Clun)-Whitcott Keysett

Start & Finish: Whitcott Keysett.
Grid Ref. SO 277824
Approx. Distance: With Clun extension — 11 miles. Without Clun extension — 3½ miles.
Approx. Time: Long — 5/6 hours. Short — 4/4½ hours.
Grade: Moderate. Muddy underfoot at times and care is needed in route-finding near Clun.
Pub/Café availability: The Crown Inn at Newcastle-on-Clun — 1 mile W. The Sun Inn and Clun Bridge Cafe at Clun — 1 mile E.

What to watch out for: In season, wild strawberries and gooseberries. Clun Castle — Norman and now in ruins, this stands on a high knoll ('otte') within a defended courtyard ('bailey') and is best viewed from the Newcastle road. It is believed to have been described in Sir Walter Scott's novel 'The Betrothed' and, with Ludlow Castle, is one of the best examples of the 150 or so 'motte and bailey' castles in the County. Prince Rhys beseiged the castle before the Battle of Radnor in 1195-6 and nearly reduced it to ashes. By 1272, it had already started to fall into ruin as conditions in the Border became more settled. Clun Church — Norman and with a lovely lychgate built in 17th C. Saxon craftsmanship is also apparent in the large, low tower. The beautiful pyramid roof and North porch are 17th C. and the font dates to the 13th C. The whole interior has a wealth of woodwork of varying ages, the pulpit being Jacobean.

1. Park SE of the hamlet of Whitcott Keysett. Take lane SE from the village and take first turning R crossing River Clun by pretty little Pontylinks Bridge.

D5

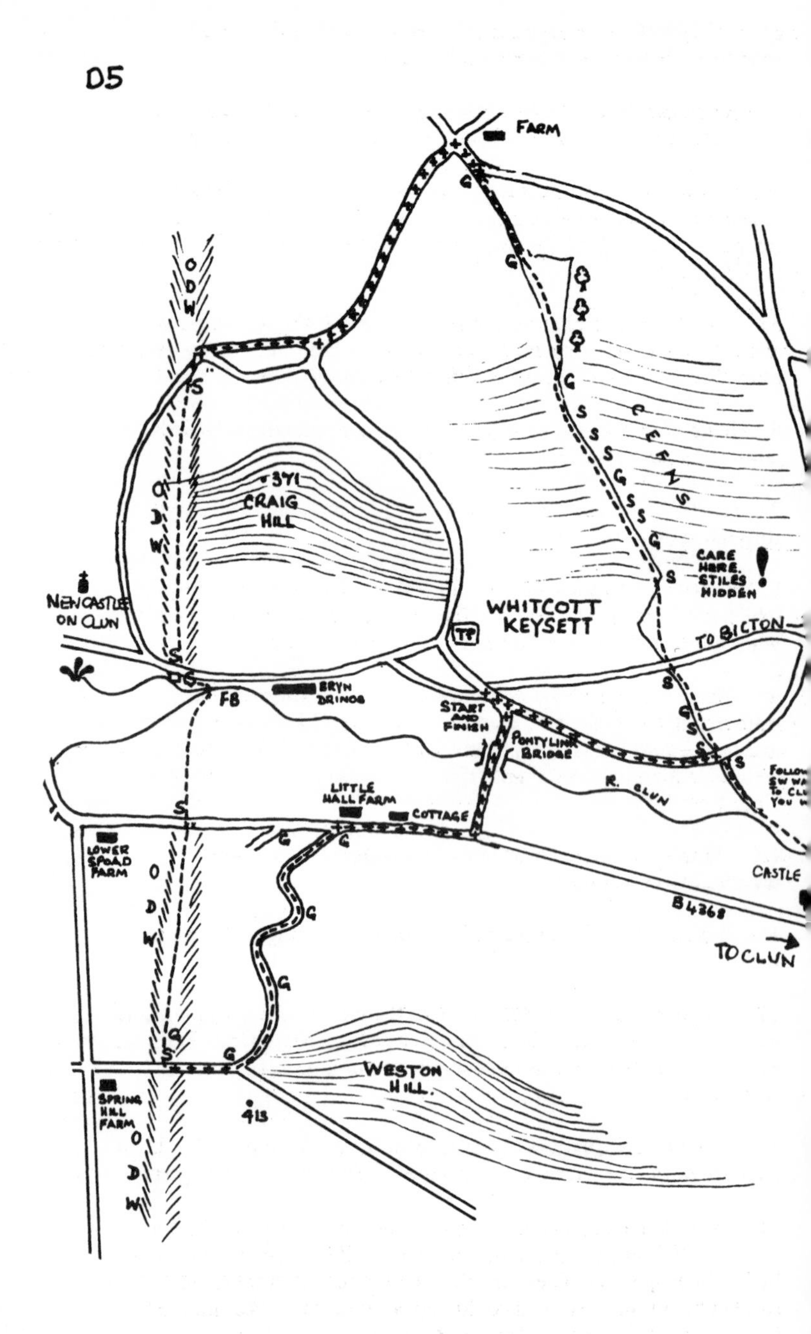
FARM
O D W
CRAIG HILL
371
C E F N S
CARE HERE. STILES HIDDEN
NEWCASTLE ON CLUN
WHITCOTT KEYSETT
TP
TO BICTON
FB
BRYN DRINOG
START AND FINISH
PONTYLINK BRIDGE
R. CLUN
LITTLE HALL FARM
COTTAGE
LOWER SPOAD FARM
CASTLE
B4368
TO CLUN
WESTON HILL.
SPRING HILL FARM
413

2. At T junction on main Clun/Newcastle road, turn R and follow road towards Newcastle for about half mile.

3. A few yards after the entrance to Little Hall Farm on your R, take first track on your L passing through a gate.

4. Follow this rising track as it winds and pass through the gates on your way until you reach a lane by a gate. You are now as near as you can be on a public footpath to the top of Weston Hill — 413 m. (1,355 ft.).

5. Turn R along high, levellish lane and savour the wide expanses all about you. Note particularly on your R, Corndon Hill; the toothy tops of the Stiperstones Ridge and the Long Mynd.

6. Just before the first farm (Springhill), take the stile on your R. This bears the Offa's Dyke path 'acorn' waymark.

7. In a few yards, go through a gate and descend the track to pass through another gate.

8. Keep in a straight line following well-trodden Offa's Dyke path which takes you along the top of the original earthwork built by others who came before us some 1100 years ago!

9. Ahead of you and down in the valley, you should see a half-timbered farmhouse — Bryndrinog. Head for this, keeping to the path and taking in the stiles and gates on your way. You pass through the well-kept farmyard of Lower Spoad Farm and reach again the main Clun/Newcastle road.

10. Turn L and after a very few yards, cross road and take waymarked stile opposite.

11. Follow the Offa's Dyke path waymarks crossing stiles and reach Bryndrinog after crossing a FB.

12. Your way is well marked through the farm buildings and up and over yet more stiles atop the ancient dyke as you climb Graig Hill (371 m. — 1,218 ft.). What this hill lacks in height it makes up for in steepness!

13. About three quarters of a mile from Bryndrinog the Offa's Dyke path crosses a lane. Here, you leave the Offa's Dyke path and turn R.

14. At fork in lane, take that to the L and turn L again at the next junction. Follow this lane uphill for about half mile passing between high, old hedgerows. These are abundant with wild flowers and raspberries in summer. You could take your mind off the climb by trying to count how many different species of plants there are!

15. At the next junction, turn R, passing a farm and when the road bends to the L immediately after that farm, you go straight on up a stony track and through a gate bearing the 'buzzard' waymark of the Shropshire Way. The stretch of walk that follows is one of my favourite 'ridge' walks in Shropshire. In mountaineering terms, to describe this as a ridge is a little like comparing Snowdon with K2, but like Snowdon. these little hills have their charm and size and height are only relative to one's surroundings.

16. Keep to a well-defined track and head generally SE. The tracks peter out at a gate to a field. Cross gate and bear diagonally L to the opposite corner of the field, climbing gradually. The open expanse here truly lifts jaded spirits.

17. After the gate on the other side of the field, follow the fence line, keeping this on your L to another gate. This type of progress follows for several fields. Do not take any gates or stiles which you may see in the fence on your L.

18. As you start to descend, your path is crossed by some pig-netting with stones on either side which, one supposes, is meant to be a sort of a stile! It may seem right to ignore this and keep on downhill following the line of your fence on the L. DO NOT. Instead, climb over pig-netting. The fence line is now on your R and thus it should remain. Remember this and watch out for stiles and gates as you descend. In particular, at least one stile is quite hidden and difficult to find, but it does exist and it should bring you out onto a lane.

19. At lane, you can either carry on to Clun or return to your start now. (If you decide to give Clun a miss, read on from No. 20). You cross lane and enter a green lane opposite. Keep in a SE direction towards Clun which should soon become visible. You take in at least three gates and cross two FB's. You should also skirt an ancient, grass-covered tumuli on your L and you enter Clun with the river on your R. From Clun, take the Newcastle road — R over the bridge — and keep to the road until you see a sign for Whitcott Keysett on your R after about one mile. This is the first lane on your R after leaving Clun. Take this, re- cross Pontylinks Bridge and return to your start.

20. Missing Clun, you turn R along the lane for half mile until you reach your start.

D6 Shadwell Hill and the Cantlin Stone

Start & Finish: Crossways.
Grid Ref. SO 204858
Approx. Distance: 5½-6 miles
Approx. Time: 2½-3 hours
Grade: Moderate. Good tracks. Little steepness.
Pub/Café availability: The Crown Inn at Newcastle-on-Clun 2½ miles SE of start).

What to watch out for: The Cantlin Stone. A flat, grey stone bearing the inscription 'W C Decsd here 1691 Buried at Betvs' and which marks the spot where, in 1691, an itinerent pedlar collapsed and died. Legend has it that he was murdered here. An argument ensued among the neighbouring parishes as to who was responsible for his burial. Finally, Bettws Y Crwyn gave him a grave in their churchyard. Nearly 200 years later, at the passing of the Clun Forest Enclosure Act, their kindness was rewarded when the proof of the Cantlin Stone gave the parish more land than originally allotted. The Kerry Ridgeway — the part of the walk from the Cantlin Stone through Long Plantation takes you along part of the Kerry Ridgeway — a way walked by human and animal feet for nearly 4,000 years! It was certainly used in the Bronze Age (2,000 BC) when in those times traders carried axe-heads eastwards and flint tools, westwards. In the late Bronze Age its use declined and the track was relegated in importance. When Offa's Dyke was built in the 8th C. the Dyke was well fortified in the vicinity of the Ridgeway and one extra fortification runs across your walk though is barely distinguishable; namely Lower Short Ditch, at the end of the Long Plantation. The track became important again in the late Medieval period when it was one of the major Welsh Drove roads. It remained thus until the 1850's when the railways finally reached the area and now its use is blessedly, confined mainly to walkers and horse- riders and forestry workers where it runs through the ubiquitous conifer stands.

1. Park near the CG at Crossways and, ignoring the lane down to Newcastle on your L, keep straight on passing Crossways Cottage on your R and a smallholding on your L and take the first turning R up a forestry track, passing a FC sign 'Ceri' on your L.

2. Keep to this rising track, passing by young spruce and fir. Another track joins you from the L. Keep straight on, passing through two gates and when the track turns R, you keep straight on along the open hilltop and along an older track which skirts the eastern contours of Shadwell Hill. Presently, away and down on your R opens high moorland hillside and as you approach conifers again, on your L near the track and surrounded by a short, wooden fence, you will see the Cantlin Stone. The trig point of Shadwell Hill is off the public footpath about 300 yards SW of the Stone and out of sight of the Stone, on the crest of the high plateau. The height here is 495 m. (1,624 ft.). The views are superb on a clear day.

3. From the Stone, continue on your track for a few yards to young forestry and pass through two gates in quick succession to enter a well-made forestry track which, fortunately at present, runs through either cleared or very young trees and affords good, open views. You have joined the site of the ancient Kerry Ridgeway Drovers Road.

4. Turn R along track and follow this high level route for about three quarters of a mile ignoring a path which leads from the R and a little later, one which leads from the L.

D6

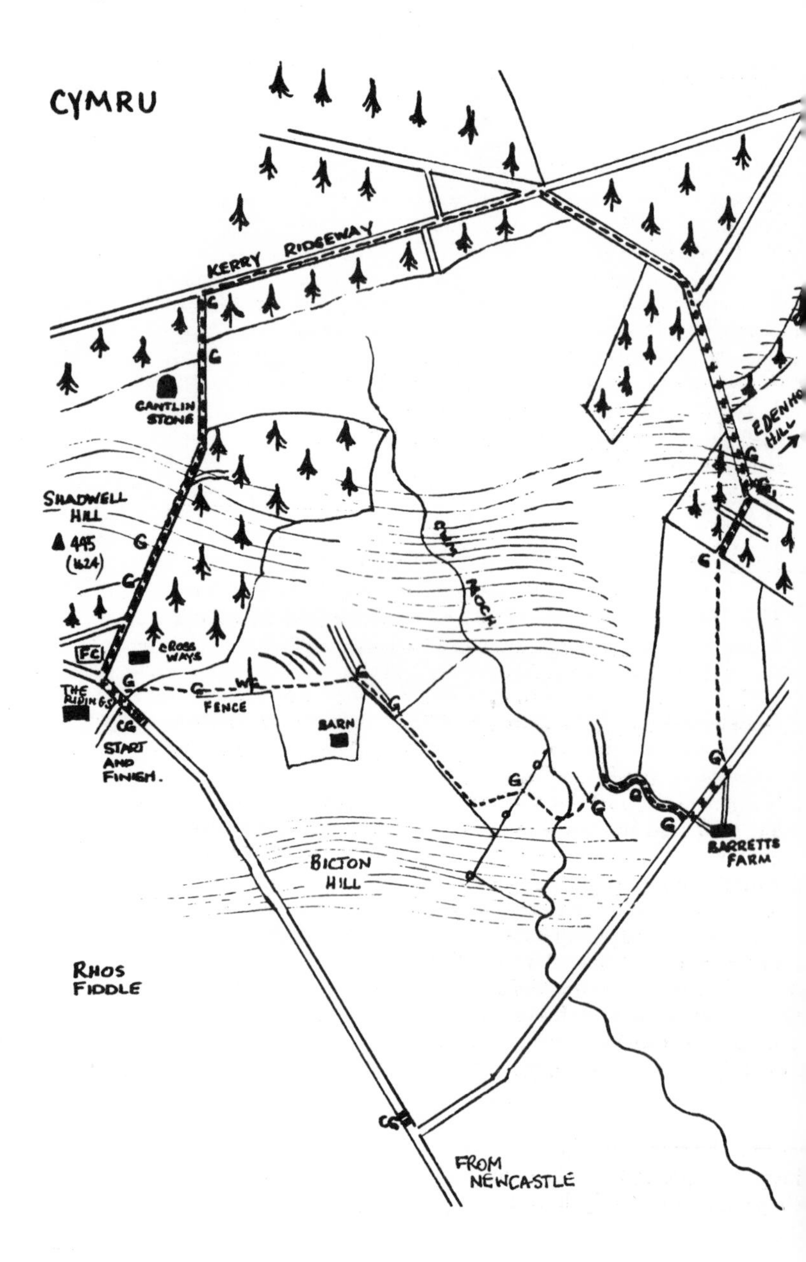
CYMRU
KERRY RIDGEWAY
CANTLIN STONE
SHADWELL HILL
445
(1624)
FC
CROSS WAYS
THE RIDINGS
CG
START AND FINISH.
FENCE
BARN
CWM MOCH
BICTON HILL
BARRETTS FARM
RHOS FIDDLE
FROM NEWCASTLE

5. When the track bears R you follow it, leaving the plantation edge and entering the woodland itself for a while but as you turn, glance L to take in the views of Stapeley Hill, Corndon and the Stiperstones.

6. You keep to this good forestry track until it joins a tarmac lane where you keep in the same line of direction, i.e. do not turn L. Again, you leave the trees and Corndon and her sisters are into view.

7. After about a third of a mile, more forestry accompanies you on your R and in another third mile — with a valley stretching below you on your L, you should see a distinct grassy 'ride' in the trees on your R. Enter this and follow to edge of trees at a gate. Below you lies a patchwork of 'Clunland'; rolling and high.

8. Cross the gate and, bearing slightly R, descend a meadow/hillside to reach the lane by a gate in the corner of the field.

9. Turn R along lane and go downhill until you reach a farm on your L. About 25 yards after the second entrance to the farm, turn R through a gate and enter an old track in a field, descending and passing through another gate.

10. Through gate, keep to track but as it winds shortly afterwards, you turn L, through a gate on your L and descend a field. Cross a stream (no FB).

11. Immediately over stream, turn R and head uphill for a gate in a hedge between two telegraph poles on your immediate skyline.

12. Through gate, bear L up the hill, across another field to reach a fence on your L. At fence, turn R and follow this — keeping it on your L — along a delightful stretch and passing through one more gate on your way.

13. Through the gate, keep the fence on your L but when you reach another gate in this fence, pass through it. You will see a large metal barn in the field you have entered.

14. Bear R away from the barn, contouring the hillside and making for some trees on your horizon.

15. As you cross the hillside, you should see a fence/hedge. Head for it and on reaching, keep it to your L and pass through a WG and two more gates in quick succession. You then skirt Crossways Cottage and enter the lane by a gate only a few yards from the CG and your start.

E. THE STIPERSTONES AREA

When you see the Stiperstones you will be aware that hills they may be, but above all they are rocks. The main ridge which extends in a roughly NE — SW direction of about 4 miles in length and which rises to 1,740 ft. is unique among South Shropshire's hill country. Jagged teeth of hard, light-coloured quartzite protrude from the high spine of the main ridge in outcrops bearing such colourful names as The Devil's Chair, Cranberry Rock, Nipstone, Shepherd's and Manstone Rock. The rock itself is, in geological terms, Ordovician — named after the Celtic tribe and was only preceded by the ancient Cambrian rock.

These hills have yielded much mineral wealth over the centuries, mainly lead but also silver and zinc. It is known that the Romans mined here as evidenced by five pigs of lead excavated which bear Emporor Hadrian's name (AD 117- 38). Lead mining declined for a while but was revived again in the 19th C. on the West side of Stiperstones from which sprang such settlements as Pennerley, Perkins Beach, Shelve and the Bog. For 150 years the area was one of Britain's main producers of lead but by 1916 this had declined to only two mines. Happily, for the sake of the hills, now only the scars remain.

As for walking; to reach the highest point — the trig point on Manstone Rock at 536 m. (1,759 ft.) — involves the use of hands. In other words a scramble. Indeed walking along the main ridge itself requires care because, although not narrow or dangerous, the rocks are hard and uneven and a misplaced foot could result in an injured ankle. On a cold, misty or rainy day this area can be quite daunting and some may even find it eerie. Indeed, in extreme conditions, Stiperstones are as inhospitable as some of the wilder reaches of Wales. A little like the Rhinog range but on a smaller scale.

Their more sinister ambience has fed colourful legend and superstition and gave Shropshire novelist Mary Webb valuable inspiration. The range was called The Daifol Mountain in 'The Golden Arrow' and The Devil's Chair itself was named. They also left their impression on earlier figures too, among them the Saxon Edric Sylvaticus — Wild Edric — who beseiged the Normans in Shrewsbury. Eventually he was captured and he and his lovely wife Godda were imprisoned below Stiperstones in 1069. Miners in former days used to say they could hear the prisoners knocking underground and wherever they knocked a rich vein of ore was found. Only when war is imminent can the pair be seen for they were then allowed to gallop over the hills until dawn when they lose their liberty again.

The walks described in this section cover not only the main ridge but also outlying hills both to east and west and although the weather can make the area seem inhospitable, the hills of and around Stiperstones offer astounding views, particularly to the west. Some people even claim to have seen Snowdon from the top of The Devil's Chair on a clear February day and towards the end of a fine evening, if you are fortunate enough to be out late, you will not easily forget the sunset. Take no notice if you should see old Satan sitting amongst the spoil of rocks. When he has nothing better to do he sits here hoping that eventually his weight will sink the stones; for when that happens England will perish. He has a long rest ahead of him!

E1 Bridges-Adstone Hill-(Wentnor)-Bridges

Start & Finish: Horseshoe Inn, Bridges.
Grid Ref. SO 394965
Approx. Distance: 4 miles
Approx. Time: 2 hours
Grade: Easy. Apart from a small section of undergrowth in summer, this walk is on good tracks and lanes.
Pub/Café availability: The Horseshoe Inn, Bridges. The Crown at Wentnor.
What to watch out for: Wentnor Church. In churchyard 'Hurricane Gravestone' bearing an inscriptiopn which reports a blizzard at nearby Asterton in 1772 which swept a house away killing seven people. The church itself contains an illustrated parchment on the wall telling its story. Originally Norman, the church was rebuilt in Victorian times using old stone.
The valley between Adstone Hill and the Long Mynd — Prolley Moor — is, according to Shropshire legend, the sleeping ground of crows and a place where witches hold midnight revelries!

1. At the 'little Venice' of Bridges, start by passing the pub on your L and walk up narrow lane passing Onny Cottage on your R.

2. Soon after the cottage, the lane begins to rise and where it turns L you leave by turning R and up a grassy track where almost immediately you meet two gates, side by side. Take RH gate and enter green lane. This charming old track contours the lower slopes of Adstone Hill with the River East Onny below you on your R.

3. Pass through two more gates and immediately over the second, carry on passing close by a hidden-away cottage on your L.

4. Past cottage, turn R but DO NOT follow on track downhill. Instead turn immediately L over a gate and enter a field.

5. In field, keep hedge on your L and cross to pass through another gate.

E1

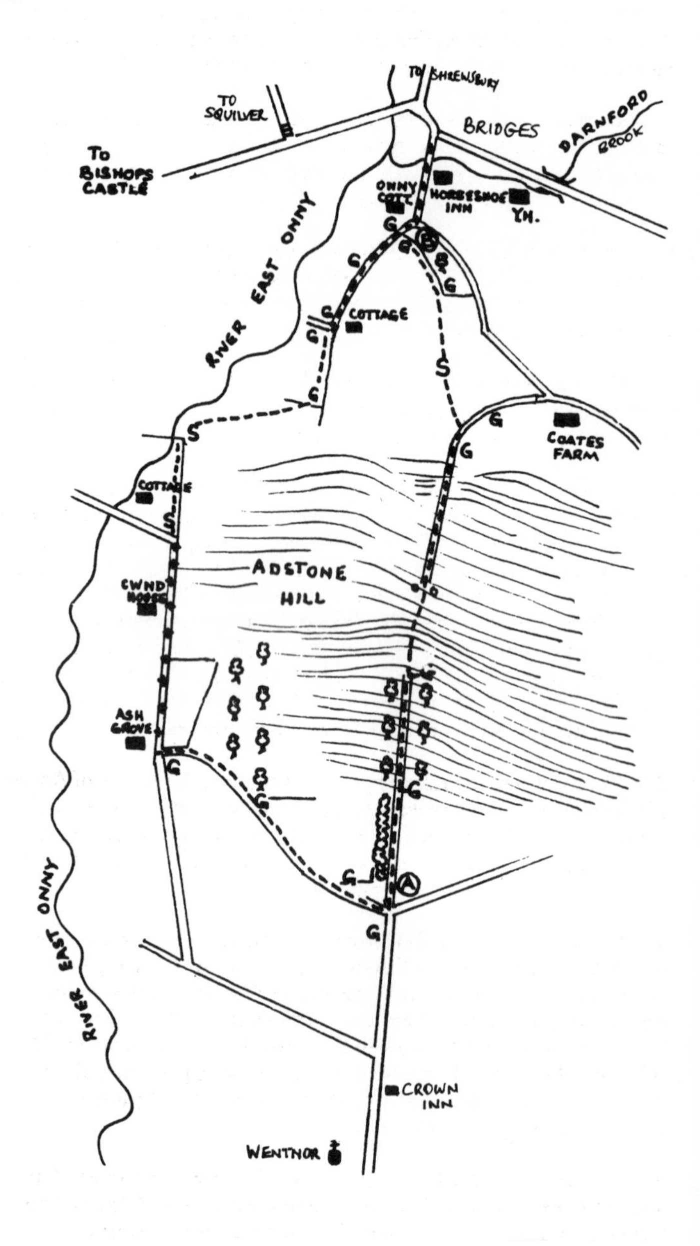

TO SHREWSBURY
TO SQUILVER
TO BISHOPS CASTLE
BRIDGES
DARNFORD BROOK
ONNY COTT.
HORSESHOE INN
Y.H.
RIVER EAST ONNY
COTTAGE
COATES FARM
COTTAGE
ADSTONE HILL
CWND HOUSE
ASH GROVE
RIVER EAST ONNY
CROWN INN
WENTNOR

6. Through this gate bear diagonally R across another field and downhill to reach a stile in corner near the river.

7. Cross stile and, keeping in the valley, (river on your R) cross next field, pass over some stepping stones in a tiny brook which crosses your path and almost immediately enter a lane by a stile. Turn L.

8. Go up lane passing two farms (Cwnd House and Ashgrove) and immediately after the latter, cross an old iron gate in the hedge on your L and enter a sunken path and climb towards some woods. This section can be very overgrown in summer.

9. When the fence on your R turns R, you follow it and although the going here is tough through bracken and bramble, persevere and keep the fence on your R ALL the time. Gradually you climb and on your way reach a gate.

10. Cross gate and enter an upland field. Still with the fence on your R but pause if you can to admire the view, in particular the delightful village of Wentnor perched on a knoll in the valley on your R.

11. Cross another gate and enter a track. In a few yards this joins a metalled lane/track. Here, you can either turn R, down lane (passing through a gate) and make for Wentnor or you can give Wentnor a miss and turn L* up a grassy ascending track. If you choose the latter, read on from 12. If you choose to go to Wentnor you will add a total of one and a half miles to your 'round trip' but it will be well worth the effort. After passing through the gate at the head of the lane, keep on this for about three quarters of a mile. After half mile it joins another lane which comes in from the R. Keep straight on and soon you reach the village. Then retrace your steps to * above (A on sketch).

12. Your way gently rises on grassy tracks along the spine of Adstone Hill. You are not high up here by most standards but this lovely hill affords some of the best views of the surrounding hills, in particular that of the Stiperstones ridge away to your L and the vast length of the Long Mynd to your R across Prolley Moor (see note).

13. On your way, you pass along a beautiful tree lined ancient green lane. At the end of this pass through a gate and rise to the top of the hill. You may see the 'buzzard' Shropshire Way waymark signs on this section. Keep in the same line of direction to the next gate from where the track bears R and goes downhill towards Coates Farm below. Do NOT take this. Instead keep on in same line along ridge over the grass (there is no well- defined path on the ground but the way is good underfoot) and soon you see a stile.

14. Cross stile and start to descend towards some beech trees. Pass by a gate and keep in line with the fence now on your R and descend quite steeply to join gate at B in sketch. Retrace your steps to start.

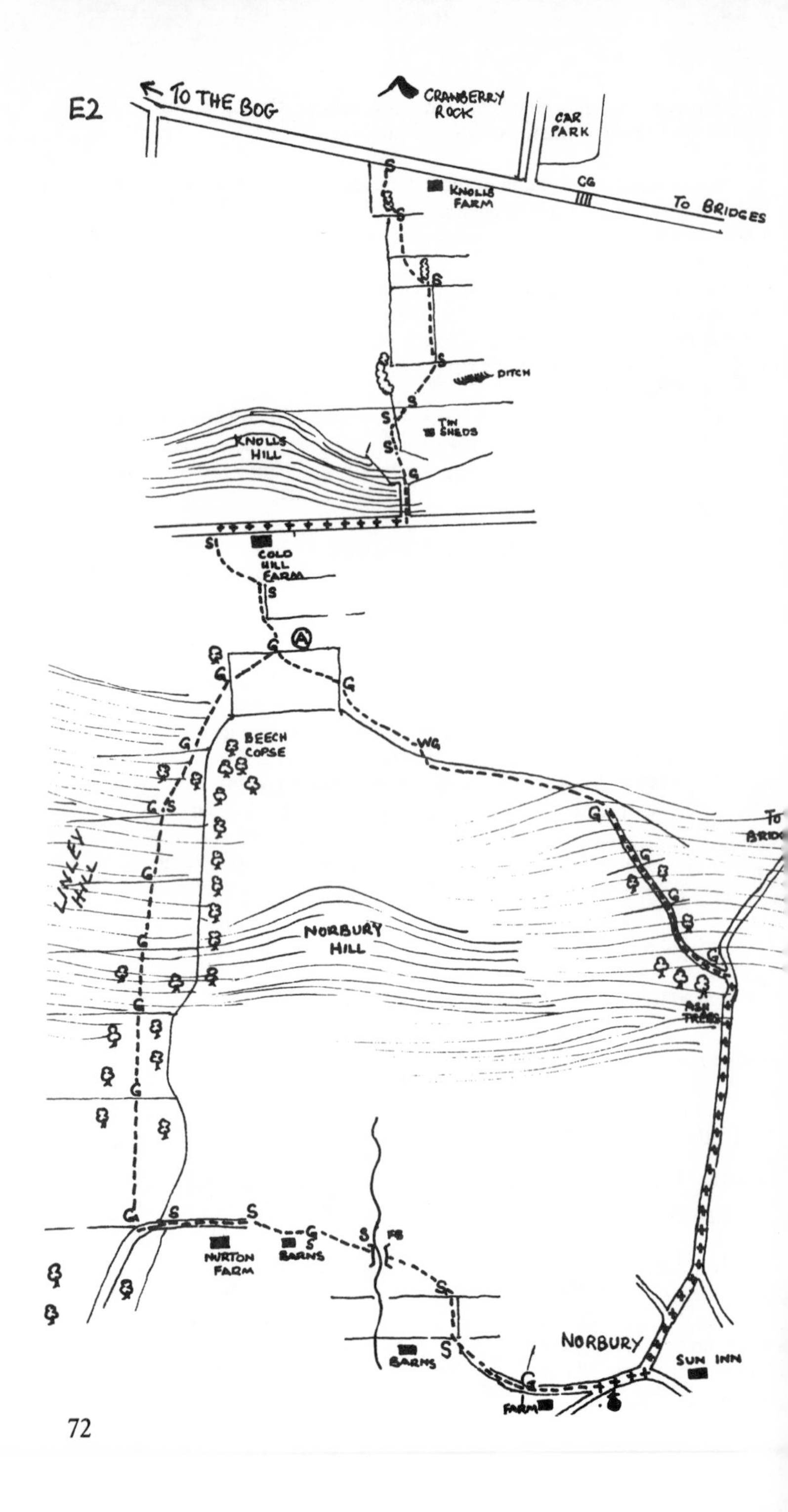
E2
TO THE BOG
CRANBERRY ROCK
CAR PARK
CG
TO BRIDGES
KNOLLS FARM
DITCH
TIN SHEDS
KNOLLS HILL
COLD HILL FARM
A
BEECH CORPSE
WG
LINLEY HILL
NORBURY HILL
ASH TREES
NURTON FARM
BARNS
FB
BARNS
NORBURY
SUN INN
FARM

E2 The Knolls-Linley Hill-Norbury-The Knolls

Start & Finish: Car Park below Cranberry Rock on Stiperstones.
Grid Ref. SO 369977
Approx. Distance: 6½-7 miles
Approx. Time: 3½-4 hours
Grade: Moderate. Generally good paths and tracks.
Pub/Café availability: The Sun Inn at Norbury — on route. The Horseshoe Inn at Bridges — 2 miles SE.
What to watch out for: Norbury Church — rebuilt in 19th C. but its 14th C. tower was then given a new shingled spire. The large font dates from the 14th C.
The ancient churchyard Yew tree, fenced in the 1790's, is one of Shropshire's finest having a measured girth in 1983 of 35 ft. The Beeches of Linley Hill. This beautifully situated avenue of trees were planted after the Napoleonic Wars by unemployed ex-soldiers. The avenue is shown on Baugh's map of Shropshire (1808) so at least part of the avenue pre-dates the Napoleonic Wars.

1. From the car park below Cranberry Rock on Stiperstones Ridge, turn R and go along the lane for about quarter of a mile passing Knolls Farm below you on your L.

2. Shortly after the farm, leave the lane by the stile on your L and enter field.

3. Descend field, keeping the hedge on your R, passing over a sheep hurdle, and veer L slightly passing through the line of an old hedge on your L, to a stile.

4. Cross stile and descend in a straight line, keeping a fence on your R.

5. Cross a ditch/stream and again veer L through a gap in another old hedge and over another stile.

6. Your way has levelled out a little now. Keep the fence on your L and follow same line to the next stile.

7. Over stile, veer R slightly and cross another ditch and head for another stile ahead of you and slightly to your R.

8. Immediately over that stile, take the stile on your R turn L and skirt the side of a hill known as 'The Knolls', the crest being above you on your R. Gradually, you reduce your height. Follow the line of the fence on your L below you. On your way, you will have good views; in particular of the Long Mynd with little Adstone Hill in the foreground.

9. When this fence ends at a gate with a stile beside it, cross stile and descend the next field, bearing slightly R to a gate. Pass through gate, enter track and shortly at the junction with the lane turn R.

10. Immediately after the first house (Cold Hill Farm), take the stile in their fence. Skirt the back of their house and cross the stile in their rear fence to enter a field.

11. Keep the field fence on your L and follow this. When it ends by turning L, you carry straight on up the hillside on a well-defined sheep-track.

12. On the crest of the hill as you look down in the same direction you have been progressing, you will see a dip below you with a sheep hurdle in a fence. Cross this and when through the hurdle/gate, ascend slightly R and make for a solitary tree on your skyline. As you approach this, more trees — a clump of Beeches — will appear.

13. At the lone tree, take the gate in the fence to the L of the tree. Follow the line of the fence now on your L and head for the clump of Beech trees.

14. When you reach the trees, look to your R to see Black Rhadley hill, Corndon and the rocky outcrops of the southern end of the Stiperstones Ridge. You now start walking along the ridge of Linley Hill itself. From the trees, having crossed the gate, keep in line with the fence on your L, passing between two more beech trees and soon you reach a stile and a gate side by side in a fence.

15. Over this stile, keep in same direction, still following the line of the fence on your L and you come to a gate and stile in the next fence. (This may bear the 'buzzard' waymark of the Shropshire Way).

16. Keep now along the ridge of Linley Hill and pass between more mature beech trees, passing through 3 or 4 more gates on your way as you descend gradually through the glorious trees. The views are beautiful and, in haymaking time, so are the smells as the scent of new-mown hay wafts up from the farms of Norbury. In the distance, lie the Brown Clee and Titterstone, making a perfect scene.

17. When you pass through a gate and enter a track, immediately turn L and cross a stile next to a gate to enter the track which passes behind Nurton Farm on your R.

18. Immediately after the farm, pass over another stile and bear slightly R towards some barns. Pass them to to their L and take another stile (next to a gate).

19. Veer L across next field and take two stiles between which is a FB over a ditch. Keep in same direction to the opposite side of the next field and when you reach the fence, turn L, keeping fence on your R and take the stile in this fence.

20. Over the stile, keep the next fence on your L and descend the next field to more barns where you cross another stile and veer left onto a track.

21. Keep on this track until you join the lane at Norbury, opposite the Church.

22. Take the first lane to the L in 20 yards (i.e. before the pub!), and follow this climbing most of the time for nearly a mile.

23. Just before a LH bend in the lane take a track on your L (there is a mature Ash tree here) and, passing through a gate, follow the track uphill by six or so Ash trees.

24. Keep to this track, ascending as you pass through three more gates. Across the valley to your L, you will see Norbury Hill.

25. Atop the hill you have ascended, you will see a gate in a fence on your R (a single gate). Go through this and follow the fence on your L until you reach the next single gate in this fence. Pass through the gate and now the fence will be on your R. You should now recognise where you left this point earlier. A on sketch.

26. Either re-trace your steps to the start or (not on sketch), after re-entering the lane at Cold Hill Farm, turn L and follow this lane (NOT turning L at next junction) to reach a T junction in about a mile. This is mostly uphill and quite steep in parts.

27. At the T junction, turn R and your start point is about one third of a mile away.

E3 The Stiperstones

Start & Finish: Cranberry Rock Car Park.
Grid Ref. SO 369977
Approx. Distance: 3 miles
Approx. Time: 1½ hours
Grade: Easy — but care is needed on rocky paths.
Pub/Café availability: The Horseshoes Inn at Bridges — 2 miles E. Stiperstones Inn at Perkins Beach — 2 miles NW.
What to watch out for: The Devil's Chair — see Introduction to this section. Also, a Nature Conservancy Council Information Board near car park at start gives further information about the area. Whinberries in season — if the sheep have left any!
N.B. *This walk can be linked with Walk E4 (see sketch) to make a good round trip of seven miles. This would make a fine walk which, in certain conditions, truly evokes the spirit of the Stiperstones.*

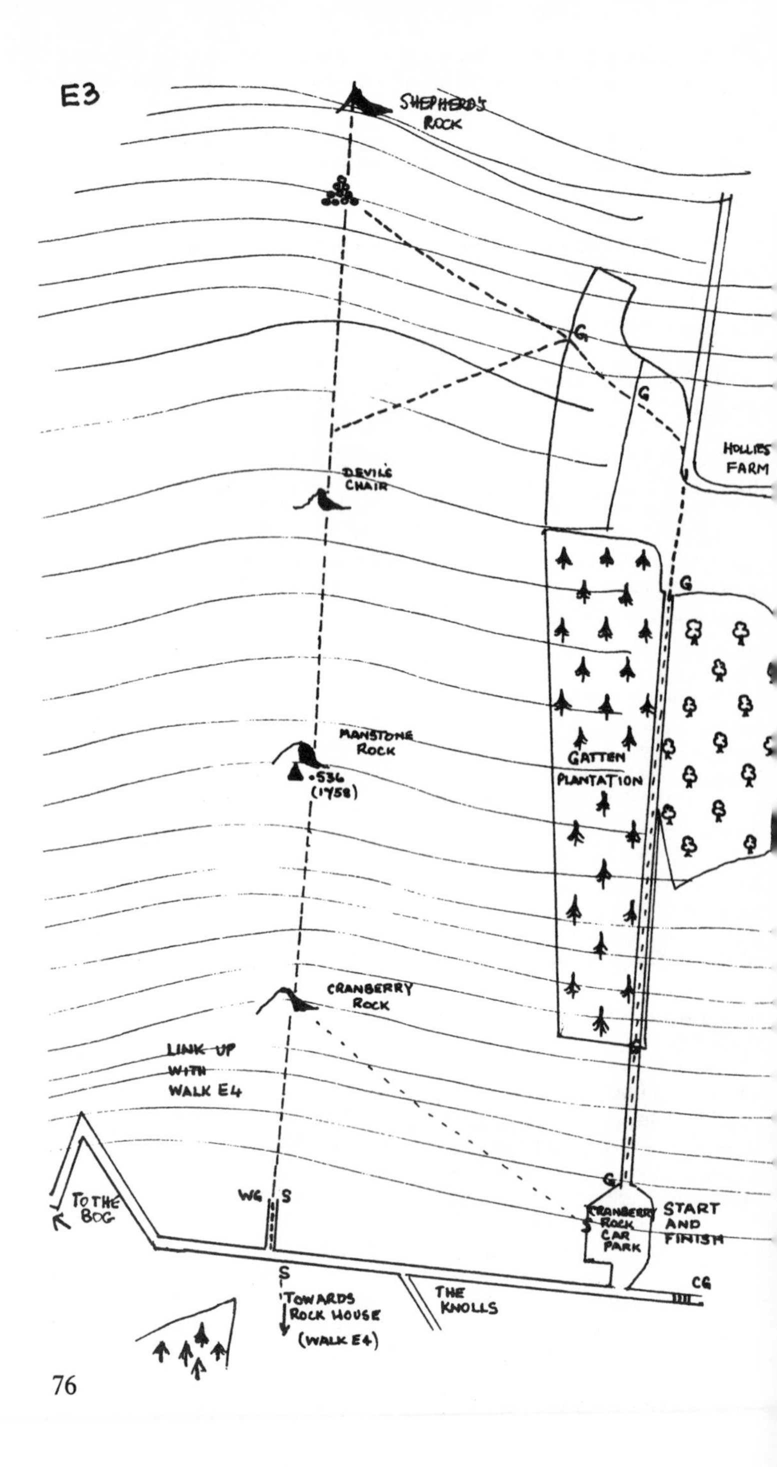
E3
SHEPHERD'S ROCK
G
G
HOLLIES FARM
DEVIL'S CHAIR
G
MANSTONE ROCK
.536 (1758)
GATTEN PLANTATION
CRANBERRY ROCK
LINK UP WITH WALK E4
G
WG
S
TO THE BOG
CRANBERRY ROCK CAR PARK
START AND FINISH
S
S
TOWARDS ROCK HOUSE (WALK E4)
THE KNOLLS
CG

1. From the car park area below Cranberry Rock and with the summit of the Stiperstones ridge on your L, take the track towards Gatten Plantation. Keep to this level track, passing through gates on your way with the trees on your L and fine open views beyond Bridges towards the Long Mynd on your R until you pass through a gate at the end of the woods.

2. You will see The Hollies Farm below you on your R but do not head for this. Instead, keep in same northerly direction across an area of meadow until you reach another track in about 50 yds. Here, turn L and head uphill towards the top of the ridge.

3. You are now on part of the Shropshire Way and after passing through a couple of gates you eventually reach the open hillside.

4. Through the last gate and when you are on the open section, bear diagonally R across the hill but towards the top of the ridge.

5. Near the top, you should meet a stone cairn and a junction of paths. Do not worry if you miss the cairn: just keep climbing until you reach the highest point and then either turn L and follow the rocky ridge-top path S and towards your start or turn R along the path in a northerly direction until you feel ready to do an about-turn S again.

6. From where you gained the ridge top, you will have superb views but you may have to stand still to enjoy them properly for when you do move, you will need to watch where you put your feet amongst the jumble of rocks rather than gaze about you.

As you progress southwards along the top, you will pass by the outcrops of jagged rocks that give the Stiperstones their 'toothy' appearance when viewed from a distance. The most northerly group is known as Shepherd's Rock; then you meet the legendary Devil's Chair; next, the highest outcrop — Manstone — with its trig offering a good scramble and standing at 536 m. (1,758 ft.). Finally, down slightly to Cranberry from where you either bear diagonally L to descend the path back to the car park or keep in your southerly direction to join the lane and Walk E4.

The views from this long ridge are nothing short of stupendous on a clear day. Distant Cadair Idris and the Aran mountains of Wales are often clearly visible and some claim to have seen Snowdon from here. Any attempt by me to describe the views would be meagre at best, presumptuous, at worst. Sample them and see for yourself!

E4

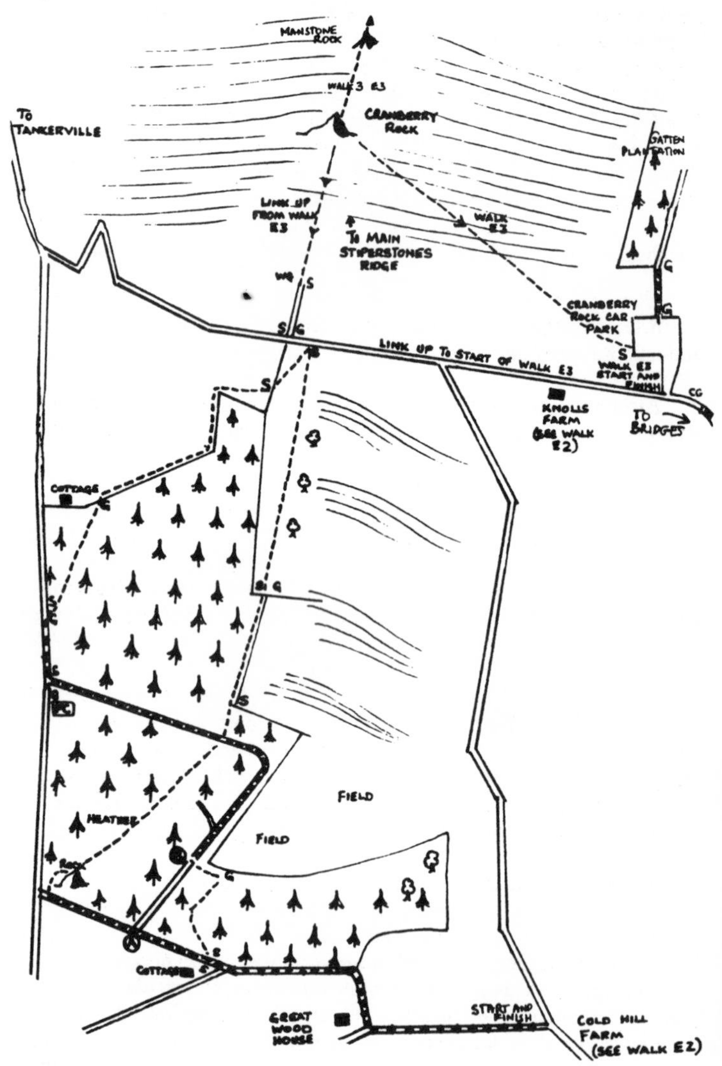
MANSTONE ROCK
WALK 3 E3
CRANBERRY ROCK
TO TANKERVILLE
GATTEN PLANTATION
LINK UP FROM WALK E3
TO MAIN STIPERSTONES RIDGE
WALK E3
CRANBERRY ROCK CAR PARK
LINK UP TO START OF WALK E3
WALK E3 START AND FINISH
KNOLLS FARM (SEE WALK E2)
TO BRIDGES
COTTAGE
FIELD
FIELD
HEATHER
ROCK
COTTAGE
GREAT WOOD HOUSE
START AND FINISH
COLD HILL FARM (SEE WALK E2)

E4 Nipstone and the Rock House, Stiperstones

Start & Finish: Near Cold Hill Farm. Grid ref. SO 364962
Approx. Distance: 4 miles
Approx. Time: 2 hours
Grade: Moderate. Steepish ascent and some mild rock scrambling.
Pub/Café availability: The Horsehoes Inn at Bridges — 2 miles E. The Stiperstones Inn at Perkins Beach — 2 miles N.
What to watch out for: The rocks on the outcrop are hard quartzite Ordovician and are 480 million years old.
N.B. *This walk can easily be linked with Walk E3 to make a fine 7 miler taking in the major part of the Stiperstones ridge and giving fine views.*

1. There is limited parking space at the road junction near Cold Hill Farm. Taking the LH fork in the lane near Cold Hill Farm follow this and head towards the wooded ridge.

2. After about half a mile, when you reach Great Wood House, take RH fork in lane. The crag-speckled wooded hillside rises above you.

3. After about quarter of a mile and just before a cottage take the nearby stile which you should find in the hedgerow on the R. Over this, follow the rising grassy path through conifers and uphill.

4. After only 20 or so yards take the path on your L, still rising and still grassy, and stay on this as it bends through the plantation.

5. When you are nearly at the top of your climb, you will see a tall rocky outcrop above you on your R. Follow path around this bearing R and now climbing over rocks in heather. The heather gives way to pure rock. Climb to top of crag, using your hands where necessary and taking care. This is known as Rock House and is the southernmost crag on the Stiperstones ridge. The views, particularly those to the East, South and West are superb.

6. Then head N along the rock-strewn path through heather along the crest of the ridge and enter the high plantation of Nipstone.

7. In the trees, the path becomes grassy and easier to negotiate but your distant views are gone for a while. However, if ever conifer plantations can be called 'lovely', this fits that description. On most days a breeze will make the trees whisper and, more often, roar and on days after rain, the grass bordering the path — of a species mostly only found in these types of plantations — is bright and a-sparkle. It is like walking on a green velvet cushion encrusted with diamond chippings.

8. When you meet a T junction and a new FC track, turn L along this and descend, now facing W, to reach the lane by a stile next to a large gate and near an FC sign 'Nipstone'.

9. Turn R and after about 100 yards, leave lane again to re-enter forestry by a stile next to a large gate and climb gradually through the trees, this time on a tussocky track.

10. You will reach a gate not far above a cottage. Turn R through gate to enter field and keep forestry fence on your R around the top end of the field. Do not take a stile which you will see in a corner of the fence leading back into the woods.

11. As you skirt the woods, Cranberry and Manstone Rocks make imposing silhouettes on the skyline ahead. Bear R around edge of woods and you will soon see a stile in a fence across field. Take this and cross next field, bearing slightly L to reach another stile at lane-edge. (This is decision time! You can either turn R and follow lane taking LH fork at junction until you reach Cranberry Rock Car Park and the start of Walk E3 OR you can continue from 12 below).

12. Do not cross lane-side stile, but turn sharp R and keep in straight line along top of field until you reach a gate and stile in fence at edge of plantation. Enter plantation by stile and follow path along edge of trees until you reach new, wide FC track.

13. Turn L and descend quite steeply. The views ahead are of the Long Mynd and Linley Hill.

14. The track turns R along bottom edge of hillside. Follow this as it levels out and until it stops! The public footpath follows the same line through the trees but is often impassable. (See A — B on sketch). You will find it easier to turn L at end of track until you reach the corner of a fence quite nearby.

15. Keeping fence and field on your L, descend steeply through the trees until you reach a grass path. (There is a gate in the fence on your L but DO NOT take this).

16. At grass path turn R and make your way along this through the trees as it turns and descends to join the path and lane you left at 3 above. On lane, turn L and re-trace your steps to the start.

E5 Mitchell's Fold and Stapeley Hill

Start & Finish: Priestweston village.
Grid ref. SO 292962
Approx. Distance: 4-5 miles
Approx. Time: 2-2½ hours
Grade: Easy. Good paths and tracks.
Pub/Café availability: The Old Miner's Arms, Priestweston. The Oak Tree Inn, Old Churchstoke — 1 mile S. The More Inn, Shelve — 1½ miles E. Cafe at Churchstoke Pottery, Churchstoke — 2½ miles SW.

What to watch out for: Stone Circle at Mitchell's Fold. A not quite perfect circle of standing stones below the summit of Stapeley Hill. Only 15 of the 30 or so original stones still stand; the tallest being about 7 ft. high. Supposed to have been erected 3,500 years ago, they are some of the more obvious legacies of the Bronze Age. (Other local evidence of Bronze Age occupation has been found at nearby Hyssington, below Corndon Hill to the S, where the remains of an axe factory has been found and was no doubt sited there to make use of the local picrite rock, a substance much favoured by early tool-makers). Yr Hen Ffordd ('The Old Way' or 'Road' in English) runs at the southern end of Stapeley Hill and was an important line of communication in the Bronze Age and for hundreds of years afterwards.

1. From Priestweston, take the lane N leading you out of the village on the Marton road. Opposite the L turning to Chirbury, take the track on your R which runs to the LH side of Priestweston Pottery, formerly a Methodist Chapel. This sunken lane climbs steadily out of the village.

2. Soon, when you join another track at a T junction turn L and shortly afterwards, by a cottage and a new bungalow, you join another, better track. Turn L along this, passing by the cottage and bungalow on your R. Below you to your L is Cwm Dingle.

3. When you reach the tarmac lane, turn L and after 50 or so yards at a RH bend in the lane, turn L onto a track. (There may be an 'English Heritage' sign in the verge on your R proclaiming — 'Stone Circle 1/4' to help you on your way).

4. Stay on this high track, enjoying the extensive views westwards and soon pass over a stile next to a gate in the track.

5. You are now on open hillside. Follow the same line of ascent — which is gradual — on a grassy path through the bracken. Soon you find yourself in the Stone Circle of Mitchell's Fold. (In an attempt to explain this creation, legend has it that during a famine, the good fairy of the nearby village of Middleton sent the villagers a cow which gave an unlimited supply of milk. The jealous bad fairy secretly inserted a sieve in the milking bucket and the cow was milked until it fell exhausted. The good fairy arrived too late to save the creature and turned the bad fairy into a block of stone, encircling her with other stones to prevent her escape).

6. From this magical spot, keep to the same grassy track and head for the first (southern) cairn on Stapeley Hill and which is clearly visible from the Circle. When this is reached, keep on in a northerly direction a short distance to reach the other cairn, i.e. that to the N. You are now on Stapeley Hill at a height of 403 m. (1,322 ft.) and you should have beautiful views on a clear day. Far away to the W you should be able to see noble Cadair Idris near the Welsh coast and nearby, the high ridge

Mitchell's Fold Stone Circle (E5)

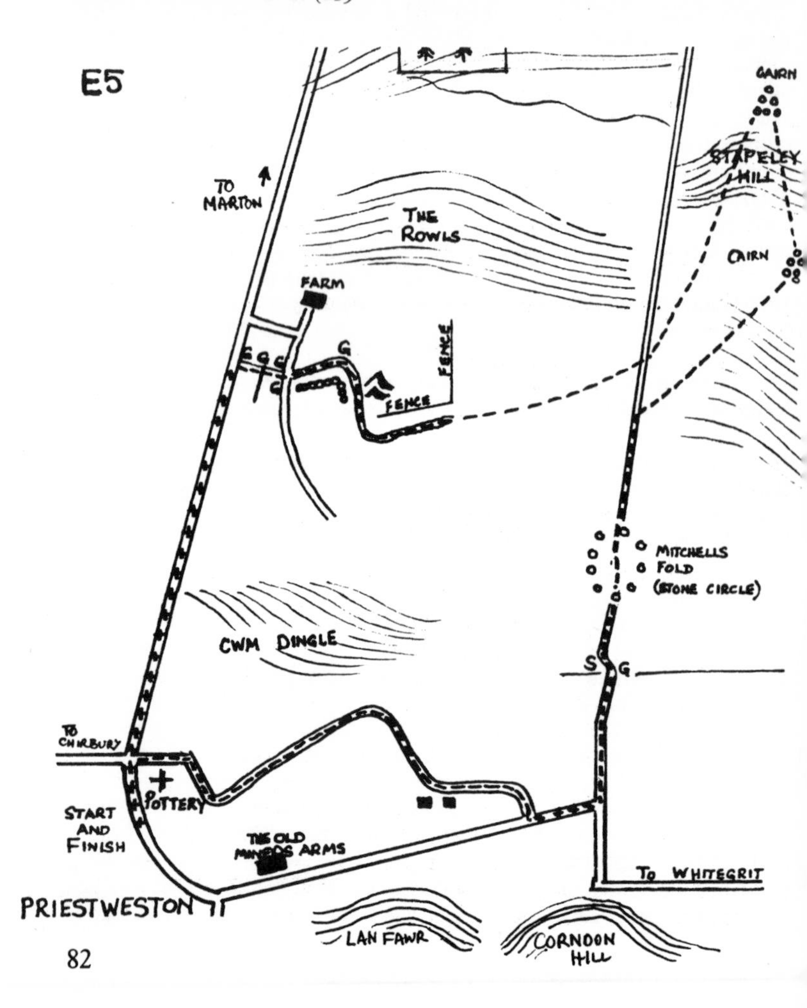

of the wild Aran mountains. Then, further N, the Berwyns while nearer is the patchwork of the valley of Montgomery with its charming town. Much nearer and to the S is Corndon Hill, with Lan Fawr to its right. To the E lie the Stiperstones ridge and its attendant hills.

7. Tearing yourself away from this glorious spot, turn back towards the southern cairn but veer away from it to your R slightly so that you descend. You will soon cross the wide grassy track.

8. Stay in the same direction, i.e. crossing the track, and head slightly uphill through the bracken but still on a grassy path, making for a fence on top of the next hill which is The Rowls. About half a mile away on your R you will see a deepish valley and a plantation. Do NOT descend this, but keep to the path until you reach the fence on the hill top.

9. At the fence, bear L so that the fence stays on your R and follow the path which widens into a track. As you walk, you will find a valley opening below you on your L. Keep to the track but when it clearly veers L, you take the fainter track R, skirting The Rowls, with a rocky outcrop slightly above you on your R. So far, you have maintained your height but now you gradually begin to descend. You join another old track by a broken down stone wall on your L. You reach a gate. Cross gate and continue on track as it bears L and soon you reach a tarmac lane which crosses your path.

10. Cross lane and take LH of two gates to enter a meadow. Cross meadow, keeping hedge on your R.

11. Cross another gate and enter and cross another meadow with the hedge still on your R until you reach a gate in a hedge on the lane-side.

12. Enter lane. Turn L and follow lane for about a mile to reach your start at Priestweston Village. The hill which now rears above on your L as you walk, is Lan Fawr. If you wish to visit the pub, take the Whitegrit road out of the village and you soon find it on your L; open for business, it is hoped.

F. TWO SMALL GEMS

The two walks in this section are within easy driving distance of each other and of Shrewsbury town. They also make ideal walks for the family. Both hills are the sites of ancient forts and are, in part, wooded. That is where their similarity ends and geologically, they are a few million years apart. Earl's/Pontesford Hill is at the northernmost end of the Stiperstones group, being composed of the ancient Ordovician rock about 400-500 million years old while Haughmond comprises the younger New Red Sandstone.

FI

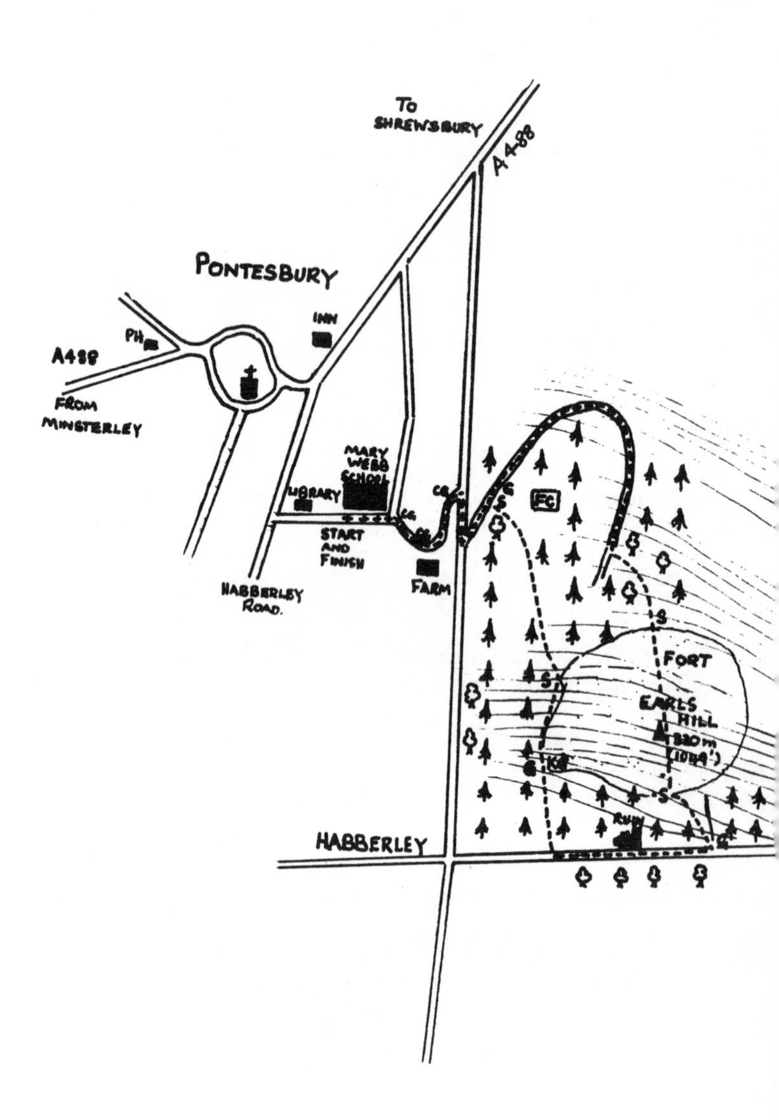

TO SHREWSBURY
A488
PONTESBURY
INN
PH
A488
FROM MINSTERLEY
MARY WEBB SCHOOL
LIBRARY
CG
START AND FINISH
FARM
HABBERLEY ROAD.
FC
S
FORT
EARLS HILL
320m
(1049')
KG
RUIN
HABBERLEY

Lovely though these hills are, it has to be said that their ascent can hardly be classed as 'hill- walking' in the more popular sense of the term. Try them, though. The views are excellent; the family will enjoy them; the leg muscles will feel that first delicious pull; the lungs will expand. In short, you will feel quite good — and the county will lie at your feet.

F1 Earl's Hill and Pontesford Hill

Start & Finish: Pontesbury.
Grid Ref. SJ 404058
Approx. Distance: 4 miles
Approx. Time: 2 hours
Grade: Easy; although one short steep ascent. Good paths and tracks.
Pub/Café availability: Two Inns at Pontesbury and a cafe.
What to watch out for: Pied Flycatcher. Comma Butterfly. Flowers — Yellow Rock Stonecrop and Bloody Cranesbill. Pontesbury Village — the home of Mary Webb the Shropshire novelist was, for two years, in a cottage here called Rose Cottage but later re-named Roseville. It was here that in 1914 she wrote 'The Golden Arrow'. Pontesbury is the site of a battle in the Easter of 661 AD between the King of Mercia and the King of the West Saxons. The church was re-fashioned in the 19th C. except for the 13th C. chancel. There are some interesting Medieval tiles depicting birds, a man and a shield. The walls are lined with Jacobean panelling and the font is Norman. Earl's Hill and Pontesford Hill Forts — these are double-banked with a ditch, sharing similarities with many other Iron Age Shropshire hill forts such as Titterstone, Abdon and Clee Burfs and Burrow Camp. Earl's Hill is now a recognised nature reserve created and sustained by the Shropshire Trust for Nature Conservation. Pontesford Hill is comprised of the ancient pre-Cambrian rock of the outcrop west of the Church Stretton fault. The hill was once the scene of a Palm Sunday custom where people would climb to the summit to look for the golden arrow which had been dropped by a king on the hill many centuries before and would only be recovered by the rightful heir to an estate.

1. Take the Habberley Road out of the village of Pontesbury and on this, take the first turning L. You can park near the Library on the L. From here, walk along the lane with the Mary Webb School on your L. About 50 yards on, with the buildings of the school still on your L, turn R down a track.

2. Follow this, crossing two CG's and after the second, turn L still along the track, cross another CG and enter the lane.

3. Turn R along the lane and in about 20 yards — opposite a marker post on your R 'Earl's Hill Summit' — leave the lane by turning L into the woods and climb up the shady track.

4. On reaching a gate, take the stile on your R. You will see a FC sign 'Pontesford Hill' near the stile and a beautiful example of a mature Spanish chestnut tree on your R. Begin to climb up the steep path rising between the trees and when, eventually, the incline lessens, keep to the path as it contours the western slopes of Pontesford Hill amidst lovely woodland. Do not leave this path and eventually you will reach a stile at the edge of the trees. High above you on your L rises Earl's Hill but it is not time to climb this yet!

5. Follow the path along the edge of the hillside until you enter woodland again at a KG next to a larger gate. (Near here you should see the information board for the Nature Reserve).

6. Shortly after the KG you meet a track at a T junction. Turn L along the track still in the trees and follow this level path (passing a ruined cottage on your L in the trees) until you reach a gate across your path. Do NOT go through this. Instead, turn L, leaving the track and taking a narrow path which rises sharply through the trees with a fence on your R.

7. At the top of the incline, watch for a faint path forking L still uphill and passing through gorse and bracken. In only about 10 yards, you will find a stile. Cross this and take path steeply uphill on the open hillside.

8. Although steep, the climb is not very long and soon you find yourself crossing the ditches of the fort's ramparts on Earl's Hill. Then, the summit marked by a trig. point. Your height is 320 m. (1,049 ft.) although your lungs may try to tell you the height is nearer that of Everest! The views are extensive from the Shropshire Plain ahead and round to the many hills of South Shropshire behind you.

9. From the summit, walk a little farther northwards and soon, below you and slightly to your L, you will see a stile at the entrance to the FC plantation of Pontesford Hill. Descend to this, cross and enter the woods. Keep to the steeply descending track through elegant, mature larch until you reach the T junction of a broader track.

10. Turn R and follow the track, descending less steeply and bearing gradually L until you find yourself passing the stile of earlier at 4 of this walk.

11. Keep the stile on your L and continue along the track to reach the lane again and re- trace your steps to the start at Pontesbury.

F2 Haughmond Hill

Start & Finish: Uffington.
Grid Ref. SJ 528135
Approx. Distance: 3 miles
Approx. Time: 1½ hours
Grade: Easy

Pub/Café availability: Corbet Arms, Uffington.
What to watch out for: Uffington — one of the disputed sites of the Battle of Shrewsbury in 1403 when Lancastrian Henry IV defeated Yorkist Sir Henry Percy (Hotspur) and which battle formed the climax of Shakespeare's 'Henry IV — Part I'. Most authorities suggest the battle took place where Battlefield Church (off the A49) now stands. The Royal Army forded the Severn here on the night of 20th July 1403, the battle, taking place the following day. Uffington Church — fairly small and re-built in the 1850's having a group of Medieval tiles and excellent old Flemish glass of which 7 panels are well-coloured and 22 are plain. Haughmond Hill — the site of an Iron Age fort on the outcrop of New Red Sandstone, Keuper marls, siltstones and sandstones. Such stone has provided building stone for such places as Shrewsbury Castle, Shrewsbury Abbey and various local churches. Haughmond Abbey — now in ruins, this monastery was a victim of the Dissolution in the reign of Henry VIII but unlike many others, this survived as a private house until it gradually fell into decline. However, the ruins still contain superb examples of Norman architecture and are open to the public:

15th Mar-15th Oct — Weekdays 9:30-1:00 and 2:00-6:30 (Sun. 2:00-6:30)
16th Oct-14th Mar — Weekdays 9:30-1:00 and 2:00-4:00 (Sun. 2:00-4:00).
Closed on Christmas Eve, Christmas Day, Boxing Day and New Year's Day.

N.B. *This is an excellent 'starter' for the potential hill-walker. Haughmond Hill is little more than a rocky outcrop from a plain but it provides a beautiful amble and takes in some lovely woodland, too.*

1. From Uffington take a track between dwellings opposite Corbet Arms Public House. Cross gate by a farm and enter field.

2. Keep in same direction across the field and head for a bridge across a rather stagnant stream: the old Shrewsbury canal.

3. Over bridge, cross next field and make for a pylon ahead, in front of which is a stile.

4. Cross stile and bear slightly R towards the pylon where, turn R along a bridle path in the trees.

5. Keep to this path for 150 yards or so. In front of you rises the rock of the hill — but you are going up the easy way.

6. When you enter more dense woodland, the path splits. One uphill and ahead, one to the R and one to the L. Take the LH path and stay with this through the trees, the edge of the wood near you on your L and the hill above you on your R. This is delightful mixed deciduous woodland of oak, ash, beech, birch and sycamore. You will probably be lucky enough to see the sudden blue flash of a jay's wing.

F2

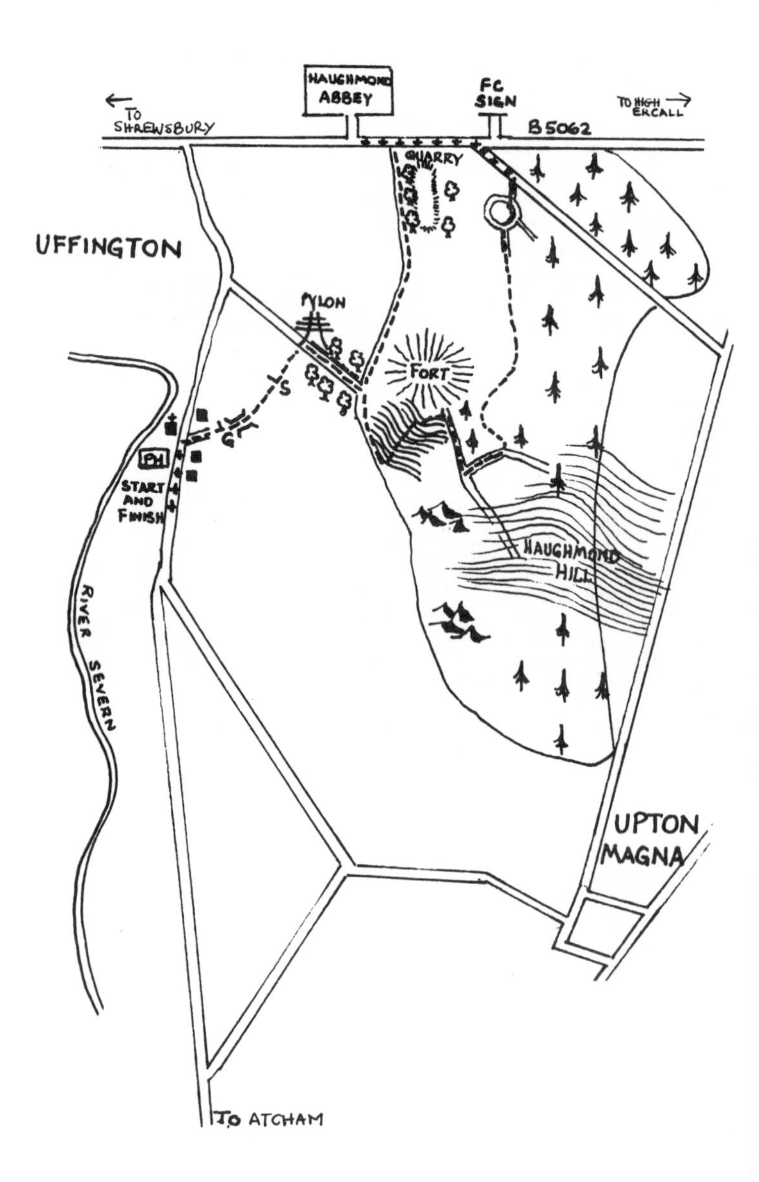

HAUGHMOND ABBEY
FC SIGN
TO SHREWSBURY
TO HIGH ERCALL
B5062
QUARRY
UFFINGTON
PYLON
S
G
FORT
PH
START AND FINISH
HAUGHMOND HILL
RIVER SEVERN
UPTON MAGNA
TO ATCHAM

7. At the end of the path and wood, if you choose to visit Haughmond Abbey, cross the main road VERY CAREFULLY. The entrance is opposite the exit from the wood. If you decide to continue your walk; out of the woods, turn R and walk a short way along the main road. (This is very busy and great care ought to be taken as the traffic travels fast here).

8. Take first turning R into a lane signposted 'Upton Magna' and after about 250 yards, turn R into woodland to enter a former car park/ picnic area.

9. Take second exit/track leading into woods from the former car park.

10. The track narrows to a path between the trees but follow this without deviating onto fainter paths which may join it. Just after passing two lightning- blasted oak trees on your R near the path, you come to a junction with a broader, grassy track among cleared trees.

11. Turn R along grassy track, which is quite level. When you reach another, better track, turn R and head for the group of Scots pine on the hilltop to your R. This is your objective — Haughmond Hill. The height is only 152 m. (500 ft.) but because it rises from a plain, you feel you are much higher and the views of the Stretton Hills and valley, Corndon, and the hills around Montgomery and Welshpool add to the feeling of height. Below you, lies Shrewsbury.

12. From the hilltop/fort, re-trace your steps for 200 yards or so until you are above a cutting in the face of the flank. This possesses the colourful name 'Lady Eleanor's Bower'. A narrow steep, but safe, path descends through bracken and briar to reach a T junction of the path along the bottom of the hill.
13. Turn R along this and follow the path until you reach the junction of 6 above, from where, turn L and retrace your steps to Uffington.

ACKNOWLEDGEMENTS & FURTHER READING

British Regional Geology
The Welsh Borderland (HMSO)
Natural Environment Research Council
Institute of Geological Sciences

A light-hearted look at our Shropshire History — Jean Hughes
2nd Edition (Wilding)

The King's England — Shropshire.
Edited by Arthur Mee (Hodder & Stoughton)

Shropshire Hills — H W Timperley
(J M Dent)

Shropshire Hill Country — Vincent Waite
(J M Dent)

The Landscape of the Welsh Marches —
Trevor Rowley (Michael Joseph)

'The Shropshire Way' — Robert Kirk
(Thornhill Press)

The Shropshire Landscape — Trevor Rowley
(Hodder & Stoughton)

Shropshire & Herefordshire Villages -
George H Haines (Robert Hale)

Walking Ancient Trackways — Michael Dunn
(David & Charles)